She WALKS in *Beauty* and ENDLESS LIGHT

ANITA KRAAL ZUIDEMA

Brilliant Books Literary
137 Forest Park Lane Thomasville
North Carolina 27360 USA

Dedicated to my precious grandchildren:

Allison, Reese, Ryleigh, Alaina, Sophia, Sydney, Scarlett

This legacy is for you and all the precious ones who follow you. Walk always in God's Endless Light. Stand up for your faith when others retreat or attack, and share your gifts with all who need your special touch.

TABLE OF CONTENTS

AUTHOR'S NOTE

I was led to revisit a classic piece of English literature, while considering the theme for this book. Written by the famous eighteenth century poet, Lord Byron, "She Walks in Beauty" awakened me to the similarities between Lord Byron's lady and the ancient Proverbs 31 ideal woman.

More than fifty years earlier, I had memorized Lord Byron's verses. Now, with a little jumpstart, I was able to retrieve several lines from long-term memory. This timely connection found a resonance that compelled me to look deeper into two poetic offerings separated by twenty centuries.

Fast-forward another two-hundred years from Lord Byron's poetic depiction of the perfect mate and here we are, early twenty-first century. On first glance, the two immortalized ladies appear old-fashioned at best, but, looking closer, we discover similarities between them and those of us who wish to be considered virtuous women, even though the world seems to have very little interest in virtue or truth.

With the encouragement of my writing coach, these two magnificent passages came together, becoming the inspiration for the book you now hold in your hands. These are the classic lines from Lord Byron:

She Walks in Beauty

She walks in beauty, like the night, of
cloudless climes and starry skies;
And all that's best of dark and bright
meet in her aspect and her eyes;
Thus mellowed to that tender light which
heaven to gaudy day denies.
One shade the more, one ray the less, had
half impaired the nameless grace
Which waves in every raven tress, or softly lightens o'er her face;
Where thoughts serenely sweet express, how
pure, how dear their dwelling place.
And on that cheek, and o'er that brow, so soft, so calm, yet eloquent,
The smiles that win, the tints that glow
but tell of days in goodness spent,
A mind at peace with all below, a heart whose love is innocent!
—Lord Byron (George Gordon) 1814—

At the same time, I was repeatedly drawn to *The Message* and its paraphrase of Proverbs 31:10–31. I decided to handwrite these virtues, hoping that would help me to bury them deep inside.

Sometime later, I wrote my own unique paraphrase, fit loosely to my own circumstances. I encourage you to spend some quality time with this lady, using the Scripture version of your choice or the paraphrase you find here. Make it yours; and make it sing for you!

Hymn to a Good Wife

A good woman is hard to find, and worth far more than diamonds.
Her husband trusts her without reserve,
and never has reason to regret it.
Never spiteful, she treats him generously all her life long.
She shops around for the best yarns and cottons,
and enjoys knitting and sewing.
She's like a trading ship that sails to faraway
places and brings back exotic surprises.
She's up before dawn, preparing breakfast for
her family and organizing her day.
She looks over a field and buys it, then, with
money she's put aside, plants a garden.
First thing in the morning, she dresses for work,
rolls up her sleeves, eager to get started.
She senses the worth of her work, is in no
hurry to call it quits for the day.
She's skilled in the crafts of home and
hearth, diligent in homemaking.
She's quick to assist anyone in need, reaches out to help the poor.
She doesn't worry about her family when it snows;
Their winter clothes are all mended and ready to wear.
She makes her own clothing, and dresses in colorful linens and silks.
Her husband is greatly respected when he
deliberates with the city fathers.
She designs gowns and sells them, brings the
sweaters she knits to the dress shops.
Her clothes are well made and elegant, and she
always faces tomorrow with a smile.
When she speaks she has something worthwhile
to say, and she always says it kindly.
She keeps an eye on everyone in her household,
and keeps them all busy and productive.

Her children respect and bless her; her husband
joins in with words of praise:
"Many women have done wonderful things,
but you've outclassed them all!"
Charm can mislead and beauty soon fades. The
woman to be admired and praised
is the woman who lives in the Fear-of-God.
Give her everything she deserves! Festoon her with praises!
—Proverbs 31:10–31(MSG)

No need to be literal in your interpretations, ladies. Choose to be a good woman, knowing that *"a good woman is hard to find, and worth far more than diamonds" (vs 10)*. Be trustworthy, generous, ambitious, and know your own worth. Use your talents to serve your family well.

You may not always be brilliant in the words you speak, but talk about worthwhile things, and be kind when you share what you know of others. Keep pursuing the virtue of being a good and noble woman.

Make your home a happy place to be. Use your time wisely and productively. With God's help, you will experience a sense of accomplishment and be energized for the future. Look beyond yourself and family and let others see and learn what it means to be a godly woman.

INTRODUCTION

When we learned Mom had Alzheimer's, she was well into her seventies. I found it easier now to blame some of her ill-chosen words and mannerisms on something other than character flaws. After she passed away, I realized my negative feelings toward some of her idiosyncrasies needed to be resolved.

Mom, as oldest daughter, had helped her own mom raise eleven of her siblings. She loved school but was often kept at home to care for toddlers, particularly when Grandma had another child. Thirteen children were born in eighteen years. They happened to be her school years. Another child meant ten days bed-rest for Grandma B and more days away from school for Mom.

While her world was rather limited in opportunities, this young girl was making responsible decisions every day. She grew up to be a very self-determined, self-reliant, and a highly opinionated lady. Mom would never have been accused of being *politically correct*.

When she gave an opinion it was truth to her. There was no debate. Counterattack was her quick serve.

I am blessed to have wonderful sisters. Five of them. They have always been (in my mind) more forgiving and tolerant of Mom's shortcomings. When we are together, we serve as one another's free counseling service. With their help I finally began to release some of my own erroneous thinking.

I grew up the oldest of eight and, like Mom, I probably took on more responsibility than was assigned to me. Now, all these many years later, I found myself praying desperately for the capacity to forgive Mom. For doing what? I really didn't know. Finally, I asked God to forgive me (this I did know) for having been so unforgiving.

I begged for answers to questions I could not formulate. I was drawn to journaling once again, often late into the night. From experience, I know that I usually learn what I am thinking by simply writing down the bare bones and then filling in the details as they fall into place.

Sitting with an open Bible in my lap, there it was! The passage in Proverbs 31 about the virtuous woman. I saw similarities I had never seen before between my farm-raised Mom and this immortalized dream woman. It came with lightning bolt clarity.

Mom was, in spite of her flaws, a very good mom who loved her Maker. I was, in spite of myself, a woman of strong faith, forgiven, and in process of being set free from thoughts that held my heart captive for much of my adult life. Like the biblical Jacob in Genesis 32, I had to wrestle with God until I was willing to beg for the blessing of forgiveness and a pure love for Mom. And yes, for myself.

When my thinking cleared, a peacefulness soothed my anxious mind and settled comfortably over me. I soon found myself writing with a new perspective and greater compassion and love for the broken vessels we are.

Once the Spirit takes hold and puts His mark on us, then God uses us to draw the world to our doorstep, and we will joyfully point to Him who is the Endless Light our souls seek.

NIGHT OWLS UNITE!

At midnight I rise to give you thanks.
—Psalm 119:62

I must have inherited Mom's midnight-oil-burner trait because I've been a night owl (or as I think of myself, a night stalker) for as long as I remember. I love to read. I love to write. I love life too much to sleep it away.

"I just need more hours in the day!" is my circadian lament.

As I started to earnestly follow His lead in my writing ventures I found that God had eased me onto a pleasant highway with countless side trips and thought-provoking lookout points. Each element of discovery leaves me thirsty and eager to draw deeper from my own memory well and other inviting fountains of life along the way.

My calling now, having reached the biblical life span of three score and ten, is to leave a legacy of thought-provoking essays and reminiscence touched with humor and poignancy to honor our family's heritage, the many sojourners I have met along the way, and the valuable lessons I have opened my eyes, my heart, and my mind to learn.

With memories revived and personalized, I aspire to leave a mealy trail of word crumbs for hungry souls to follow till they find themselves seated at a bountiful table of healthy ideas and discourse.

"I now know who I am and what I am supposed to be doing," I whisper, to no one in particular.

I found similar words attributed to several different authors, and they resonate with my own experience, but an unknown *he or she* penned my thoughts best: *Since I've owned my calling to write, I've experienced more freedom and joy than at any other time in my past.*

For every sleepless hour repurposed to tell the stories, my constant companion is the One I diligently seek so I may enjoy His presence in my life. When I finally head up the stairs and crawl under the covers, I am in a much better state of mind than when I crept downstairs to begin yet another midnight writing marathon.

So, yeah for us, night owls! We are masters of "doing what our hands find to do" (Eccl. 9:10) even in the wee small hours of the morning. Even if others, or we ourselves, think we've lost our minds.

I am so glad you are here. I pray you will experience God's presence in your life as we walk the path together toward the endless light of His love.

Something to Ponder

- Are you an early morning riser or a night owl?
- How does this affect your ability to accomplish your life-sized goals?
- Is there a tidbit or two from what you've read that encourages you to fight on, or do you need a new action plan?
- Start journaling about your life and where you find yourself. Go back occasionally, read and see how you've grown!

Walking in My Daughter's Footsteps

She speaks with wisdom, and faithful instruction is on her lips,
She watches over the affairs of her household,
Her children rise up and call her blessed.
—Proverbs 31:26-27

Determined moms of preschoolers (MOPS), all aiming to park as close to the door as possible, struggle to unload and rearm themselves with baby in heavy car seat, an exuberant preschooler or two in tow and possibly a hot dish to pass.

It is snowing heavily on this single-digit frost-bitten morning, but precious time with women friends is worth all the effort it takes to bundle everyone up to escape the norm on this MOPS Tuesday.

I am parked on the far end of the parking lot between daughter Amy's van and the *paper gator*. Only the two of us are parked this far out. Amy, on staff, is asked to park on the perimeter. Me? I have papers to unload. I also came to play the piano for the preschoolers but am so invigorated by the sun glistening on the fresh snow that I can't resist a little extra walk time.

I heft the heavy newspapers into the gator and take the first few snow-covered steps, breaking out into a smile as I realize, *I'm walking in Amy's footprints!*

I head toward the door, a million memories floating through my mind. I thank God once again that we worship and serve together with our entire family in this well-loved place.

It has been nearly twenty years since our family began an odyssey that took us through the refining fires of grief and sadness.

Our daughter Alicia lost her husband and first love on Thanksgiving Day of 1994. He died of a sudden heart attack at our home. Jerry was twenty-five and precious to all of us. My dad died less than three weeks later on December 11. Pancreatic cancer was his stalker.

A short time after Dad's death, my mother went through an unexpected, but successful, surgery for colon cancer. We felt blessed and comforted.

Within a year, my husband Al's mom fell into a coma while vacationing in California. Al and I flew to be with Dad and his siblings and spouses to gather around her hospital bed. We were there for a week before she was taken to her eternal home.

Earlier, I was knee-deep into my thesis for an M.Ed in Learning Disabilities, determined to complete over Christmas break. Now, all the gathered data and copy sat forlorn and out of sight. It would be two years before I held the completed copy in my hands.

As a family we found ourselves in a cataclysmic world of grief. But, through the storms of loss and deep sadness, God was always faithful and He brought us to a new realization of His endless love for us and for our family.

Through the ensuing years I found myself learning many things from my two young daughters. Today, I see strength of character found only in those who have been tested at a deeper level, who not only survived but learned to thrive.

We had walked many miles together through dark days and slogged through deep valleys. We shared good times and new lessons of faith, and in His time all things were made new and even beautiful again.

When I come back to a car warmed by a winter sun, I decide to put in writing what it has been like to observe my daughters as they mother their own children in a world far less safe, more conflicted, and never void of danger. Quite unlike the world they knew as children.

It is a difficult but vital role today's mothers fill, teaching their children how to be light bearers in the world they will grow up to serve.

Full-time mom, Alicia, works a few hours each day as *lunch lady* at daughter Alaina's school. We laugh at some of the stories of the personalities and antics she deals with in the lunchroom and on the playground.

When she first considered this position I remember saying, "Why not? She definitely has the right stuff: a positive attitude, a warm and sun-drenched disposition. She makes friends easily. She isn't afraid to make decisions and has good judgment. The kids will love her!"

Both daughters have church and school responsibilities in addition to all the mom stuff with kids in four seasons of sports. Both women also love their time at home with their kids and faithfully anticipate the end of every school day.

I remember it all so well. Funny how both daughters seem to be internally programmed to the school bells ring.

As they ponder the afternoon snack are they remembering the smell of fresh-baked cookies or brownies waiting for them and their friends? Do they remember furiously talking over one another sharing the highlights and tragedies of the day before they ran back out the door to play?

Today is report card time. We have happy grandkids with great reports—confirming their moms' persistence with the daily challenge of homework.

I thank God my girls delight in mothering as I did so many years ago. As I watch, I learn. I learn what it takes in today's world to be a virtuous Proverbs 31 woman.

I stand proud to have raised good leaders and faithful servants. They walk in beauty and God's endless light.

Something to Ponder

- What character traits do you admire most in the young women you know best or meet along life's path?
- If you have daughters who are mothers, or sons who are fathers, focus on what you admire most about their parenting skills. What have you learned from them or from other young parents who you admire?
- List some of the struggles faced by women today, unfamiliar to past generations. Do the same for men. Where can we turn for wisdom and answers?
- Write a cheery note to someone who needs encouragement in the difficult role of parenting, whether alone or as a couple. Share your delight in something that has encouraged you.

Follow the Yellow Brick Road

I press on to make it my own,
because Christ Jesus has made me his own.
—Philippians 3:12 (NRSV)

I never knew money could be used for anything but bottom line essentials. I didn't feel the need for more as a young country girl. None of our friends or family had the finer stuff of life. I wouldn't say I thrived, but I more than survived.

Other girls had cute outfits and jewelry, maybe a fancy haircut or even new saddle shoes, but I was well-grounded and knew that someday my parent's aspirations would come full circle for me, their firstborn child.

I had much to learn but, because of them, I owned a strong work ethic and had great faith. Anything less than success was unacceptable. I had no idea what success meant, other than doing your best in school, at work, on a mission trip—wherever.

Mom and I were excited one early September morning. It was 1963, and we saw the Welcome to Knollcrest! sign. Only freshmen classes and housing were offered that year on Calvin College's newly built campus. A girl's dorm, a guy's dorm, a dining hall, and a library-classroom—that was our campus. It was all about function.

The unique setting and ambience that is Calvin today with tree-lined, fully landscaped paths was not realized until much later.

I'm sure Mom and Dad had no idea how this was going to work financially. Five of their eight children were already attending Christian school. Dad was a factory worker for most of his life. Mom worked nights at Heinz Pickle factory during canning season and many more years at the laundromat next door to where she got her hair done for the week.

The sliding scale for families like ours who struggled with the high costs of Christian education could only carry them so far. We relied on summer produce, corn and pickles for tuition money. No one was exempt from the labor force.

Mom and Dad, with years of wisdom and lots of prior opportunities to grow their faith like they grew vegetables, simply relied on God to carry us through each new chapter of life.

I had never seen *The Wizard of Oz* (1939), and I am sure I did not connect the dots from Dorothy's life to mine at age eighteen. Calvin College proved, however, to be my yellow brick road, and I would follow that path through thorns and briars, distance and time, back and forth from hope and despair, success and failure, for several decades.

Later that freshmen year, I took the commuter bus to Calvin's Franklin campus for a popular philosophy class with upperclassmen friends. We often shared a large, round table in the Commons after class. Most of them were men as I recall. We met for coffee. I had no spending money, nor did many of them. We really just met to talk and philosophize about life in the real world.

We chatted amicably over topics of the day, and philosophy assignments given by an eccentric but brilliant professor with so many driving mishaps his license would soon be revoked. We debated politics and theology, usually at high decibels.

I truly enjoyed the broader perspectives of my new, academically oriented, friends. We laughed often. And loudly!

My world was expanding in ways I couldn't have imagined as a country girl from a small town, and I welcomed it with an invigorated and voracious mind.

On my way to German class that infamous day, November 22, 1963, we were stunned into silence and then awash with tears as we heard the schoolwide announcement that our beloved president had died, victim of the unconscionable act of assassination.

President Kennedy's death affected us deeply, and we shed worrisome tears and shared fears for the future of an America we thought had gone crazy, and was still at war. But we were young, naïve, and optimistic to our roots.

The Vietnam War, ten years along its continuum (1954–1975) was very real for classmates who had recently come of age. We debated the pros and cons and spoke in hushed tones of classmates and family members who were in the service, some who came home in body bags or suffered permanent scars, internal and external. We knew their names. We knew their young faces.

The world was insane, but it was exciting too. In spite of our innocence and ignorance, we all grew up a lot that fateful year.

We admired Jerry Ford, our hometown hero, and were encouraged by his continuing bid for congressman from West Michigan's Fifth District.

I was there when he stopped at the college on one of his trips home to Grand Rapids. He knew he could expect an accommodating but heated debate on the issues of the day. He enjoyed the exuberance of our company, and we loved and honored him in return. He spent time shaking hands and then sat down at our table to lead us in a healthy discussion on foreign policy and our military involvement in Vietnam.

His polished dress shoes were propped up on the table, his ever present pipe glowed in his hand, and peach brandy smoke circled the table and mingled with the pipe smoke of the other men in my world.

Ten years later, many of us would hold *our Jerry* close in prayer as he took the solemn vows to become President Gerald R. Ford of the United States of America, following a troubling Watergate scandal. I believe God used Calvin students to help President Ford firm up his conservative principles and guide him spiritually through rough terrain as he led a badly wounded nation back toward moral stability.

I loved my life as it was then. It was never easy, but we were young and invincible.

Time, however, changes everything, and my world was about to change as well. The yellow brick road would fade from view, but I know now that I never left the path as I pursued life as a young wife and mother committed to Christian school and church ministry.

God was faithful, and with a clearer vision, I returned to my alma mater at age thirty-eight to finish the college education I so treasured in my teen years. At age fifty, I finally achieved a master's degree in learning disabilities.

I had already accepted the challenge to set up and administer a program for learning disabled students at Calvin Christian High School, in our hometown of Grandville. It was the place where our children had learned to love God, to serve others, and to value good principles for living with a world and life view.

That pathway had led to a place in my life, more than any other, which gave me fulfillment and great satisfaction. Full of ruts and deep ravines, but the tried and true path was always there for me to follow. Today, it beckons still, even as I slow the pace. I press on toward the goal, the same prize that kept Paul energized till the end of his earthly life, knowing the end is only the beginning.

Something to Ponder

- Is there someone in your past or present, who serves as a valuable influence in your life today?
- How does God fit into the frame-work of your life?
- Are there goals or dreams from childhood that followed you into adulthood? How do they impact your life today?
- Is it time to make a new start? Or, should you keep the faith and maintain the resolve to finish the race and achieve your goals?

Life Lessons from a Dream

In a dream, in a vision of the night, when
sound sleep falls on mortals ...
He opens their ears ... and terrifies them with warnings,
That He may turn them aside from their deeds and keep
them from pride.
—Job 33:15–17 (KJV)

I came home all fired up! I planned to contact everyone I'd ever talked with about my home-based business. I loved the products. I absolutely believed in the health benefits. My vision was clear, my mission strong. I would not be stymied in my commitment to succeed. I would be positive in every downturn or facing any battle with myself and with others. I was determined to succeed in this last bigger-than-me venture before I retired.

That evening I quietly recounted how God had given me new purpose for living many years earlier. I had prayed every day for answers and a way out of the sedentary lifestyle I was forced to live.

I loved life. Sitting in a faux leather recliner as a young mom of young teenagers with unrelenting back pain and never-ending headaches was totally contrary to what I wanted to do with my time and my life. My beautiful daughters deserved more. My faithful husband did not deserve to come home to vacuuming and cleanup duties.

Unbelievably, God met my request in an unusual way. I learned about prolotherapy from a neighbor, and after completing two years of what is now called regenerative injection therapy, I knew I had been given a precious gift and a new start. I set out to finish the bachelor's degree I left dangling at twenty years old.

With determination, Al's and mine, I graduated at age forty-two with a music/education major. Twice the age of my classmates, I felt doubly blessed that God had *restored the years the locusts had eaten away.* (Joel 2:25).

I was hired to teach music at Potter's House, a mission-based Christian elementary school where I had interned earlier. In that special place I was able to fulfill another dream of using my education in a mission setting.

I loved the culturally diverse student body and wholeheartedly confirmed the creative methods of teaching encouraged by a young and ambitious principal and mission-minded staff.

Soon, by an amazing twist and turn, God nudged me to pursue certification in learning disabilities. This pointed me in the direction of several short-term positions within the Christian Learning Center schools. I learned much in regular and LD classrooms at the elementary and middle school level.

Soon I was led to take a part-time CLC position at Calvin Christian Middle, and by the time I completed my thesis for a master's degree in learning disabilities, I was nearly fifty years old and had successfully launched the Academic Resource Program (ARP) at Calvin Christian High. Those amazing and appreciative students gave me much love and satisfaction in return for all the effort put in to meet their individual needs.

I had joyfully served the teaching profession for about fifteen years when the career path ahead took another unexpected turn. This time I sat with my superiors in conference to discuss the growing concerns of the ARP and the financial hardships our school was facing.

I was asked to find a way to cut staff and student caseload, while we were all aware that the demands of teachers, parents, and students were for increased services, not less. I knew immediately what my answer would have to be.

"Someone else," I said, "will have to be that person."

I had heard God's voice. This time at great personal and financial sacrifice. A few months later, I said good-bye to the students I loved and the program I had birthed.

The summer of 2003 was spent in quiet resignation. I had no heart for going back to the job market in my field, so the future was unknown. I had loved being "Mrs. Z." I was proud of the program and what we had achieved. Who was I now?

Without the title for which I worked so long and hard, the reason for getting up in the morning, and my identity, seemed forever lost.

That fall, a formidable health and wellness company had been a godsend and the perfect fit for someone like me with a teaching background. I was successful for the first seven years, but now my health was consuming more of my time and energy.

I loved sharing stories about the health advantages of our products, but actual sales management became increasingly more difficult. More and more, the business was about the latest gadgetry or social media tools—all necessary in today's business climate but foreign to my tool kit. My simple business venture morphed into something I had no desire to pursue.

When I looked in the mirror, an uncertain and irresolute woman stared me down once again. I saw the reality of impending age and the results of not being aligned to God's will for my life.

The business I began in order to improve my health had given me a new sense of identity and joy, but the price it was exacting was too high. That was the reality I had persistently ignored.

Before dawn of the next morning, something occurred I will never forget.

I woke with vivid recollections of a remarkable dream. I knew immediately that God was giving me a new vision and new goals.

I got up, settled into my favorite chair, and let my mind traverse this timely dream at a deeper level. I was stunned by the clarity of the images seared into my brain. I knew it had meaning for me at this unsettled juncture in my life.

> I stood on the ledge of a mountain range, jagged peaks and treacherous rocks all around. I had tediously climbed to this point without injury and was eager to resume the climb. The mountain peaks above were silhouetted in striking shades of blue and purple. I was soon carried mindlessly upward by the grandeur all around.
>
> At the highest peak, I gazed in awe of a panoramic scene and was amazed how far I had travelled. Then I peered over the rocky and craggy edge. Fear, paralyzing fear, took hold.
>
> A peacefully protected valley surrounded by a placid, crystal clear lake extended as far as I could see. It shimmered in the sun, more beautiful than I can put into words. I longed to explore this new world.
>
> Next, my mind's eye took in the images of healthy and active people of all ages surrounded by friends and family. There was laughter, joy, and there was love. A visible love of life and all God's gifts.

Contentment and peace radiated from that valley like a sweet field of flora. How I longed to join them.

Before I could start the menacing climb downward, however, I knew I would have to release a lot of lingering uncertainties and fears.

I would have to act with boldness and self-confidence to propel myself over that foreboding ledge. The twisted, vine-covered descent would be treacherous and uncharted.

In desperation, I looked around for the easiest route with the least amount of risk.

I also remembered a feeling of fearful exhilaration and was encouraged by the welcoming shouts of those enjoying life down in that dreamlike valley. It sent jolts of energy and purpose through my veins!

Then, from far below, I clearly heard someone calling my name, saying, "Trust God, Anita, and let go of your fears." Those exact words.

As I sat in pensive mode, I recognized clearly what I would experience in my life if I finally decided to give up my own fearful imaginations.

I knew God was greater than my fears, that He was forever faithful, and that *His compassions were new every morning* (Lam. 3:22–23). It was clearer still that the joy of serving Him was all I needed to carry me safely into the future. James tells us He was and forever is the God who goes with us through every unknown (James 1:2–4).

God has the blueprint of our lives written firmly on the palm of His hand. He knows and will direct our steps along the very best route possible. Not necessarily the easiest, but the glory will belong to God while the increase of our joy for living will be unmeasured.

> *For I know the plans I have for you … to*
> *give you hope and a future.*
> —Jeremiah 29:11

Something to Ponder

- Has a dream ever disrupted your future plans? Did it change your thinking in a good or bad way?
- As a writer, I sometimes say, "I learn what I really think when I take the time to write it down." Try it! Take a backward glance through your life.
- Name the various places, people and ideas that have brought you to the lookout point where you stand today.

MIDNIGHT MADNESS

<><><><><><><><><><><><><><><><><><><><><><><><><><><><><><><><><><><><><><><>

Her Lamp does not go out at night ...
Her hands hold the spindle.
—Proverbs 31:18–19

Imagine the time absorbed with hand-smocking the bodice of a gingham Sunday dress. Mom was a pro with needles. It was a relaxation technique for one like her, running to keep up with the clock all day. More than once, she sewed and then smocked big and little sister dresses, alike except for color choice. I know much of this happened after the midnight hour.

Prior to each Tulip Time in Holland, Mom would be busy creating and sewing Dutch costumes for anyone in her family who was in the parade, or in later years, for my younger sisters who performed as klompen dancers every year. Specified costumes under specific rules. Mom lived life under the gun at this time of year. The only hours left to claim would be the midnight hours, which often morphed into all-nighters.

She would carefully set, cut, and then pin pattern pieces together. Finally her beloved sewing machine would hum alongside her precious radio with WJBL's late-night meditations, sermonettes, *Songs in the Night*, and finally, *The Haven of Rest*. The theme song drifts easily to mind after all these years: "I've anchored my soul in the haven of rest, I'll sail the wide seas no more. The tempest may rage (or was it roar?) but in Jesus, I'm safe evermore" (Henry Lake Gilmore, 1836).

Mom's little radio buddy kept her company and wide awake through the profitable midnight hours, but WJBL sometimes ended with a white noise snore before Mom found her pillow in the predawn hours.

When I think of the effort involved to prepare and serve meals and then attack the cleanup process with her growing brood circling round, the fact that we were exceptionally healthy kids is a credit to God's grace and Mom's vigilance with food management as well as her willing and ready spirit to work late into the night.

For all her worth, Mom never had the opportunity to make an executive decision, such as, "Tonight, we are eating out!"

Our meals were never anything but wholesome. Junk food was, well, junk that other people ate. Canning summer's bounty most often demanded the midnight oil. But it also meant her family was well supplied through dark and long Michigan winters. I don't remember Mom ever complaining about too little sleep. As long as God was with her, she had everything she needed for the next day's adventures.

Something to Ponder

- If you have to "make up for lost time," do you prefer the midnight hours or the early morning hours?
- Who's your "buddy" for these lonely hours? (Ear buds, coffee, chocolates, dog,...)
- Don't forget Him who promises "to be with you always, to the end of the age." Here on earth now, and as we transition to our new life in heaven to be with Him forever. (Matthew 28:20)

Bringing Beauty to Our World

She looks well to the ways of her household
and does not eat the bread of idleness.
—Proverbs 31:27

My nine-year-old granddaughter, Sophia, loves to do dishes. At least for now. Her eyes light up when she learns she follows a long line of smart women who actually enjoy doing dishes. She knows I love to wash my baking and cooking utensils by hand rather than load up and later have to empty the dishwasher. The hot, sudsy water is soothing as it warms and relaxes my senses.

Sophia's Great-Grandma Kraal was my mom. Born into a busy farm family, Ann never owned a dishwasher till late in life. Her responsibilities, with eleven younger siblings, were numerous, but cooking and cleanup for fifteen had to be the most repetitious and time-consuming. And invariable, as she became mom to eight of her own.

We, her girls, thought she dawdled too long at the sink, prolonging the process by talking too much. Wanting to expedite and evacuate, we would offer to finish up, but she would simply say, "I love doing dishes!" And, "It's the best way to clean my fingernails." No argument there. We also wanted clean nails, Mom! And a quick finish!

When Mom and Dad finally built a home near the creek on their beloved twenty-five acre minifarm, she wasn't much interested in a dishwasher. Shar, Ruth, and Deb, teens still at home, were vocal and instrumental in helping Mom see the sensibility of this necessity.

Why, I wonder, do I still enjoy this mundane activity? Is it just because I am the oldest daughter, like Mom—responsibility oozing out of every pore? Was our world so small, my expectations so limited, that I found satisfaction in places peculiar, even surprising?

Then, why do some in my daughters' generation of overtaxed and over-extended mothers still enjoy, as a general rule, these and other repetitive chores?

Driven women, clearing away the morning's clutter after kisses and hugs and the last door slams. Today. Tomorrow. Repeat! Forget the chef hat or the calico apron. Mom is frantically chopping veggies and chicken to fill a crock-pot.

The smell alone will brighten her day when she returns home. Mopping up spills, undoing bathroom calamities, returning messy to springtime fresh, with never a minute to waste!

But take a moment and look again. The lady takes a fleeting glance around. She quickly moves to adjust the lamp shade a centimeter to the right, stands back, and looks around one more time. There's a distinct and contented grin.

So, what is that expression? I think it is a godlike, "Behold! It is very good!" Satisfaction, another divine gift, propels her forward to the next messy.

And when she steps outside her door, she becomes God's gift of beauty to the needy and messy world around.

Something to Ponder

- Is there a chore or job that seems mundane or even detestable to others, but you, however, enjoy? What's your reasoning?

- I hope you're journaling along with us and finding new ideas to cultivate and advance your own life's story.
- Proverbs 31:27 says, "She (he) looks well to the ways of her (his) family and does not eat the bread of idleness." Do you find it hard to measure up to this standard? Do you want to roll over on the couch and hit the snooze button, or are you inspired to get out there and produce—for your family, your Maker, and for your own self-worth.

HEIRLOOM ORNAMENTS

*Does a young woman forget her jewelry, or
a bride her wedding ornaments?
Yet, my people have forgotten me, days without number.*
—Jeremiah 2:32

I was touched in an unusual way this morning as I read from Titus 2. Paul speaks to slaves who are part of the household of faith. He tells them to be submissive to their masters and give satisfaction so that *in everything they may be an ornament to the gospel of God our Savior* (Titus 2:10 ESV).

The Message commissions us as slaves of Jesus Christ to let our good character shine through our actions, *adding luster to the teachings of our Savior God.* Isn't that a great image?

I was drawn to the word *ornament* because I had just finished trimming the Christmas tree downstairs with my Precious Moments and Hummel ornaments. As each is lovingly taken from its box, stories of how they came into our possession are remembered or retold.

Personalizing our stories helps the younger ones value what will someday be passed down as heirlooms to add luster and import to their own Christmas traditions.

Adding luster is also the principle behind staging a house to show value and uniqueness by the way it is dressed and ornamented for the occasion.

I have pearls and matching earrings that have been worn numerous times by family members for weddings or special events. I share them happily as a personal blessing on that person.

In the same way, jewelry passed down from grandmother to daughter, granddaughter, or someone loved reminds the receiver of blessings being passed along from one generation to another. It belongs to an heirloom of valued memories.

Our own significance as lustrous, shiny ornaments should increase with age and direct association with the One we call Master. We have the opportunity to add irresistible beauty to the gospel message by the wisdom we share in our words and actions and how we present ourselves to the world around us.

Scarves, jewelry, nail polish, makeup, faux or classic jewelry, appropriately used, may serve to draw people to us. It is truly up to us to be an attractive and beautiful ornament to Him who has purchased us with the price of His own blood.

As a treasured bride of Christ, our desire should be to please Him. The reward awaits.

They (the saints) shall sparkle in His land like jewels in a crown.
How attractive and beautiful they will be!
—Zechariah 9:16b

Something to Ponder

- What are some of the words you were drawn to as you read this essay? What feelings rise to the surface as you read it again?
- Does God love beauty? How are we to show our love for Him?
- How do the words: ornament, luster, heirloom, jewelry, shiny, attractive, treasured, sparkle... help you to understand how Christ feels about us, His Bride? How should we reciprocate His love for us?

Surviving or Thriving

<><><><><><><><><><><><><><><><><><><><><><><><><><><><><><><><><><><><><><><><><>

Jesus looked at them and said, "With man this is impossible,
but with God all things are possible."
—Matthew 19:26

I listened to the breaking news story of a young woman in our area, physically and psychologically bloodied by the abuse and rejection of one she trusted and loved. My heart grieves. How can anyone recover from such personal violation?

Cancer has become an everyday occurrence for far too many of our friends and family. The carnage is enormous from a physical, emotional, and psychological perspective. The loss is often so great, and the road to recovery so steep.

A friend of mine was brutally mauled and raped at knifepoint many years ago. Her goals and direction in life were forever altered that day.

These are not rare stories. The scenarios are never quite the same, but the effects can be seen and felt for a lifetime.

While you are reading this essay you might be reprocessing some dark event of your own, or that of someone you cared for or loved. Strong in faith, weak in faith, or no faith at all. Life is never without pain and suffering.

Some experience psychological scarring for life, living with bitterness, unresolved anger, and shame or paralyzing fear. Some harbor an unforgiving spirit toward the perpetrator. Sometimes, we feel as though we have only God to blame.

In spite of deep, penetrating wounds, some find the will and the courage to overcome and live again, mentally and spiritually healthy. My friend shares her story to offer hope and encouragement that life can and will be good once again. Life for her is life lived in Christ. She is alive and thriving.

There may be scars. Ugly scars. Invisible or visible. We might even be driven to face the finality of life—for ourselves or for someone we love.

We recently attended a funeral of a young man who was loved by so many. We wondered how his parents would survive the horror of his sudden death. But we are believers, and we know the truth. His parents will survive, not without pain or scars, but they will experience God's grace and sufficiency.

Look back over the years. How do you see the scars of your life? Are you bitter? Angry? Unforgiving?

Or do the scars serve as reminders of God's compassionate and healing power in your life? Are you stronger today because of the obstacles you overcame in the past?

If the answer is yes, you are living out the legacy of this important truth: attitude is always a choice.

You have learned the wonderful secret of how to thrive, not simply survive the inevitable storms of life. You will be able to look back and acknowledge that you have matured in all the right ways.

Attitude is more important than the past, than education,
than money, than circumstance, than failure or success …
We have a choice every day regarding the
attitude we will embrace for that day.
We cannot change our past. We cannot change the inevitable.
The only thing we can do is play the one string we have, and
that is our attitude.
—Author unknown, attributed to
Reverend Charles Stanley.

Something to Ponder

- From past experience, do you see yourself as a survivor or as someone who not only survives but has also learned to thrive?
- Why do some reject God's healing power for the future and hold tight to anger and bitterness?
- What does attitude have to do with surviving or thriving?

IN THE WEE SMALL HOURS
OF THE MORNING[*]

Be careful then, how you live, not as unwise people but as wise,
making the most of your time, because the days are evil.
—Ephesians 5:15-16 (NRSV)

These forages into the late night or predawn hours might just be my favorite time of the day. I relish the quiet stillness with no interruptions.

My brain clears of the fog created by too much stimulating activity all day, circumstances that cannot be altered in my life, politics or news reports that only seem to get more bizarre.

When I can't sleep, I slip down the stairs, fix a cup of chamomile mint tea, and settle into my comfy reading chair. I'm happiest when I can wrap up in my wintertime throw, but it is early autumn, so I resist the thought.

I pull out my floppy faux-leather, large-print Bible from the overflowing basket alongside my fireside reading chair. I smile each time I pick it up. I had my eye on that Bible long before Mom died. Its position on the faded seat of her sewing chair, at home and later in her Royal Park condo, never changed.

---

[*] *In the Wee Small Hours of the Morning* (1955), a collection of ballads arranged for Frank Sinatra by Nelson Riddle.

Mom spent many of her later years as a volunteer for Bibles for Mexico, later renamed Bibles for Missions. She would occasionally spend a few dollars on things she thought were worth more than the tag indicated.

This Bible had drawn her attention at some point, and mine, every time I visited. As the oldest of the sibs and most visually impaired, it seemed meant for me. Furthermore, there were no contenders.

The first page was torn away, so neither Mom nor I knew the first owner, But, there were many verses highlighted that told the story of a life lived at peace with God and with life itself.

I hike up my aching feet onto a favorite footstool and start searching the concordance for a specific passage on the invisible foe I'm facing this ungodly hour.

Fear, anger, or anxiety are common sorties for me. This activates my mental Bible memory app, and soon my unsettled mind relaxes peacefully and begins searching for sleep mode. I say a prayer of thanks, and usually I am set to head back up the stairs.

Tonight, though, I'm feeling some urgency about the Lifelong Learning class I'm taking, so I pick up that mentally hefty historical novel I'm trying to get a handle on. I have another seventy pages of *The Brothers Karamazov* to read before my discussion class, tomorrow morning.

The story is intricately constructed, full of knotty twists and turns. I know next to nothing about Russian history, and I am ashamed to say, I know even less about this world-renowned author. Fyodor Dostoevsky also authored *Crime and Punishment*, and who hasn't heard of that daunting masterpiece? More shame surfaces as I admit (only to myself) that I haven't read that one either!

The Brothers Karamazov is a story of three brothers from three different mothers. There is an in-depth analysis of each character within the dynamics of a dysfunctional Russian family similar to Fyodor's real-life family.

I muse. What interest might there be in telling the stories of a *functional* family? Who could relate? Fortunately, there aren't many of those, so it must be helpful to us who come from dysfunctional families to learn from a genius such as Dostoevsky as he struggles vainly to unravel and decode the craziness from which he came.

By creating this mastermind story, he reaps the therapeutic benefits of unraveling his own congested thinking and we, his fortunate readers, therein find our own peace.

Therapeutic benefits! Now that is an eye-opener I can agree with completely! And an inspiring thought as I begin to test the wind currents as a writer, caught up with the mission of writing for legacy and advancement of God's kingdom here on earth.

Dostoevsky is universally recognized for focusing on two fundamental questions in all his writings: What do human beings owe to God? And what do human beings owe to others? A worthy premise; one I find myself pursuing daily. Sometimes with an aura of guilt.

A few days ago, I listened as Dennis Prager and Charles Krauthammer (notable thinkers and authors in my day) conversed about how *The Brothers Karamazov* shaped their thinking into the remarkable people they are today.

Amazing, the timing of this drop-load of intelligence! I love these guys! So now I have resolved to gather whatever crumbs or droppings I can find under the table of this noteworthy classic.

I manage to cover another ten pages, more confused than before. Doubts swirl around me, but I refuse to give up ... not yet, at least.

This convoluted and complicated novel has not been conducive to my winding down, and it is now 1:30 a.m. I drop the paperback down on the coffee table and pick up one of the women's magazines piled high and mostly untouched.

My singular goal now is to catch up quickly with what's current in the world around me and maybe even find another best-ever recipe to cram into an already overstuffed box.

Being involved with higher education for so long, I have very little taste for pleasurable drivel, so after a few minutes I'm bored enough to go back to bed. Mindless foolishness, oh, how sweet it is!

Something to Ponder

- Do you have pressing issues that keep you awake in the darkness of night? Make a list. Is it fear? Anger? Worry? Injustice in the world or around you? Insecurity about the future?
- Name it all before God in prayer.
- Accept God's healing power over you and yours. Pray believing, then, give it to him. Go to bed and sleep like a baby.

METAMORPHOSIS

Every day of my life was recorded in your book.
Every moment was laid out before a single day had passed.
— (Ps. 139:13–16 NLT)

It's quiet this morning as I swing gently back and forth. The lake is blue-green, flat, and calm. The breeze is gentle. My neighbor, in his little fishing boat, hauls up what looks to be an undersized bass. Over it goes. Not big enough yet for the fry pan.

A monarch butterfly circles round, skitters in and out of the flowering peach blossom astilbe along the garden wall. A variety of birdsongs add to the glow of a new day. The devotional I'm reading settles further into my lap as I allow myself to reflect on the monarch's brief lifespan and how we correlate. Soon I begin to contemplate the monarch's and my own metamorphosis. From birth to prime time ... the *now* of life.

Later that day I am writing about something unrelated, but I can't let go of how this intricate gift of nature, the magnificent monarch butterfly, helps me to understand my own transformations. Created miracles of a grand designer, we both experience multiple transformations before we fully mature.

We begin as fertilized eggs, but our lives soon take divergent paths. Our transformations will be unique in scope and significance. Walk with me along this remarkable path, and see yourself as God sees you. The psalmist says this about my beginning and yours:

You made all the delicate, inner parts of my body.
You knit me together in my mother's womb.
You saw me before I was born.
(Ps. 139: 13-15 NLT)

The caterpillar stage is amazing to study. At its onset the caterpillar is minute in size, sometimes invisible, but by DNA she is programmed to eat. And eat she does!

A truly voracious eating machine, the caterpillar can increase in size a thousand-fold within a period of several weeks! The caterpillar must shed its skin or molt several times to accommodate its emergent size. (No analogy here, please!)

Very soon it must find the right leaf for its express dietary needs in a place where it will be safe and can spin a chrysalis. Transformation takes place here.

The outside of the chrysalis may appear restful, but inside there is an amazing new creature being formed with tissue, limbs, and organs. One would have to admit, this is Transformation with a capital T! At completion, the butterfly emerges and within hours begins its "freedom flight."

Transformation from caterpillar to butterfly is amazing in scope but purely physical in nature. The story is quite different for humans, created in God's likeness. We grow from infancy to adulthood, mentally, emotionally, and physically, but transformation is most often about an inner makeover and that happens in the heart.

Transformation is a choice we make for ourselves. We often call it our "personal growth and development" stage. Paul reminds us from his own experience:

Let God transform you into a new person
by changing the way you think.
Then you will learn to know God's will for you ...
Be honest in your evaluation of yourself,

> *Measuring yourself by the faith God has given us.*
> (Rom. 12:2–3 NLT)

The choice is mine. It's my decision to choose to allow the Spirit of God to carry out a complete transformation of my character, my will, my whole being, to fundamentally change who I am and make me new, to *consume me from the inside out so I may love (Him) from the inside out.**

More than ten years ago, I was encouraged to write a life-purpose statement. After many attempts to present myself in a good light, I got down on my knees and humbly asked God what He wanted from me. Here is my simple statement of faith that leads me on and forward today.

> *To mirror on the outside*
> *What God has shaped me to be on the inside.*
> *A loving and faithful servant,*
> *A passionate ambassador of authentic joy and peace,*
> *Bringing hope and healing, making a difference wherever I go.*

Like the caterpillar losing her skin, I have learned to loosen my grip on things or passions I'm reluctant to give up, knowing that if I refuse, God has no problem finding other ways to get my attention!

Nearly every position I have held has been unique or uncharted. I don't think of myself as a risk-taker, but each time, God has placed His hand on me and sent me to an arena where a leap of faith is required and transformation is inevitable.

Like metamorphosis taking place in a chrysalis, life goes on, but inside, God disassembles me to the core. In His time and in His way the pieces come together as only He can envision.

---

* "Cry of my Heart" Terry Butler, 1991, Mercy/Vineyard Publishing, Hillsong United.

Looking back, I can affirm that most significant transformations in my life take place after a time of intense and often painful inner struggle. That too is by design—God's design. Slowly, light breaks through, and I discover I have grown into my new skin. Once again, it's a new day, and I'm ready for my "freedom flight!"

> *See, I am making all things new!*
> —Revelations 21:5 (NRSV)

Something to Ponder

- React to the statement "Transformation is a choice we make… " (top of pg 33)
- How does or doesn't this statement mesh with the Scripture verse that follows from Romans 12:2-3?
- Would you agree? It's our choice to change and to be transformed but we first need to "learn to know His will" (thru prayer, Scripture, life events…) and then pray for God to give us courage and will-power to change the way we think and act.
- Do you have a faith statement and, if so, how does it affect your life and give you assurance for the future?

FREEDOM FLIGHT

◇◇◇

We are God's workmanship, created in Christ Jesus to do
good works, prepared by God, in advance, for us to do.
—Ephesians 2:10.

By their very nature, butterflies bring joy and beauty to the heart of God. They are, of course, only one of many natural wonders He blesses our lives with every day.

To those who choose His will as a guide for living He gives the added gift of true *inner* beauty.

We know these gifts as *the fruit of the Spirit.* Together, *love, joy, peace, patience, kindness, goodness, faithfulness, gentleness, and self-control* (Gal. 5:22) are to be spread around to brighten and enlighten weary souls wherever we stop to bless, just as the butterfly leaves precious pollen wherever it goes.

I want to be like the amazing butterfly that does her work quietly but effectively, demonstrating grace and beauty, looking continually for the right place to infuse the *fruit of the Spirit.*

Here are some simple and fun facts I learned about the monarch butterfly and the implications I drew for my own life.

○ Butterflies are meant to fly and pollinate wherever they go. *We are commissioned to bless others and make disciples wherever we go.*

- ○ Butterflies need the sun. A little warming and they are ready to fly. *The warmth of His Word and Spirit warms and inspires us to spread joy and love all around.*
- ○ Dragonflies and birds eat large numbers of caterpillars. *Don't mess around. Get to the butterfly stage before you are eaten alive.*
- ○ Butterflies have wingspans of up to eleven inches. *What is my potential wingspan? Or how wide is my outreach?*
- ○ Monarchs head to warmer climes before winter. *Some species are smarter than others. Hmm!* (It is January. Having left Michigan on December 31, where would you guess I am now?)
- ○ The lifespan of a butterfly is one month to a year. *Life is short ... Don't waste a moment!*

Something to Ponder

- • What fruit of the Spirit might others see as your most obvious gift(s) as listed in Galatians 5:22 (pg 36, 3rd paragraph).
- • What fruit or gift(s) of the Spirit do you see in yourself and enjoy most? Pick a bouquet if you like! Focus on the gift(s) you've selected and highlight it (or them) for the world to see.
- • Which fun fact (bullet point) did you especially enjoy and relate to?

READY OR NOT

See, I am making all things new! Then He said to me,
Write this, for these words are trustworthy and true. It is done.
I am the Alpha and Omega, the Beginning and the End.
—Revelations 21:5–6 (NRSV)

The essay *Metamorphosis* was scripted several years ago. As I reread the piece with editing eyes, I came to the realization that God had programmed in yet another transition, this time for Al and me together.

Weaseling our way through a difficult season of stress and instability over the last few years, we were well aware of being caught in the crux of a major transition. Retirement was real, irreconcilable, exciting.

Having lived our lives purely as worker bees who functioned independently for the greater part of each day, we knew how to give one another space and time. To dream it and do it. Late in the day we would meet comfortably somewhere in the middle, most times on the family room couch.

Last year and this, Al closed up his business and painfully cleared out drawings and business manuals, computers and paraphernalia gathered from five decades of mechanical engineering. He also cleaned out years of a do-it-yourselfers basement, including his dad's do-it-yourself collection of tools, nuts, bolts, and screws. All the while he volunteered as facilities manager for a large renovation project at our church.

The catalyst to our latest and greatest transition was the sudden purchase of a newly roughed-in condo we stumbled over on a drive-by after church one Sunday. Exactly where we were meant to be.

What fun we had selecting appliances, cabinetry, colors, finishes, and furniture for the space we knew would be perfect for our slower lifestyle. Having the responsibility of self-contracting twice before, Al was ready to let go of the attending annoyances. This time, our builder had all the headaches while we had all the fun.

We had lived our lives with too much to do and never enough downtime. Now, suddenly, everything is different. We are learning to blend two very independent lives and give each other space while pursuing new ventures and enjoying a cup of afternoon tea, guilt free.

With less responsibilities, I have more time to write and no more excuses for not completing this project.

Initiated as simple legacy memoir for family, it has evolved into something far more challenging. With encouragement from friends and family I am now in a full out sprint to complete an undertaking begun more than five years ago.

What I thought would be impossible now stands in tribute to the One who makes it all possible. In His time and in His way.

Something to Ponder

- What transition(s) in life has impacted you the most, in a growing sort of way?
- Have you ever been forced to deal with an unwelcome transition in life? Name it for yourself and then think about whether there were any positives that (later) you

could thank God for carrying you through the hardship of that experience?

- Is there a project or undertaking you have been avoiding and making excuses for? Reawaken the dream and take step one.

THE HANDS OF A PROVERBS 31 WOMAN

Give her a share in the fruits of her hands and let her
works praise her in the city gates.
—Proverbs 31:31 (NRSV)

Grandma B stands at the time honored cast iron sink, dozens of eggs piled high in a basket set on an old but sturdy chair close by. The eggs are still warm from the henhouse. She has on a clean nondescript house dress, calf length, covered with a tiny floral patterned apron, common to all the women I know.

Grandma knows I dislike going into the henhouse to collect the eggs, but I do enjoy helping her clean those yucky things and getting them ready to sell so we can buy more groceries. Why did I like that smelly job? I wonder if I just liked spending time with this mild mannered lady who was always there for me. Together, we would carefully wipe the eggs clean with a soft, wet rag before layering them gently into flats, each holding three dozen ready-to-move beauties.

Cooking and baking was in progress nonstop at Grandma's house. Peanut butter or molasses cookies or a frosted cake consumed in one road-worthy coffee break for unknown quantities of hungry farmhands at ten and three o'clock. Homemade bread never made it to the bread pudding stage.

As I write, I muse. I'm amazed at the fortitude and the inner strength of women like my grandma. How did they accomplish so much in a twenty-four-hour day? My kids would say, "No cake or frosting mixes? No microwave oven? No Frosted Flakes or instant oatmeal? No Zip-loc bags or Tupperware? And then, what would my own list tell about me?

Grandma was generally cheerful, and I think she enjoyed her life, maybe even when cleaning dirty eggs or scrubbing blackened and baked on pots and pans. *No Pam. No nonstick teflon!*

Brillo pads, seven daughters, and occasionally I, firstborn granddaughter, were the only maid-service Grandma ever knew. No Alaskan cruise to dream about while whittling away at the stack of mending heaped high by her favorite rocker.

Imagine the tower of dishes Grandma B could have washed and stacked in her lifetime. When I was young, there would have been one or two Chatty Cathys standing by to wipe or stuff the dishes and utensils into overflowing cupboards and drawers.

Subsidiary kitchen jobs lurked for any laggards or dawdlers. Women also served as extra farmhands, so some of them would happily skedaddle to the barn.

(Reciprocity on the men's part, helping in the kitchen or with the children, was not commonplace until much later.)

I remember Grandma B mending overalls and darning socks as soon as she sat down, late in the evening. Not an occasional *What-shall-I-do-now* activity. It was an *every-time-I-sit-me-down* necessity. She kept the family's clothes in good repair so they would hold together a little longer and still be wearable for the next in line. No such thing as throwaways.

For many of Grandma B's brood-raising years, all clothes, pretty Sunday dresses, and farm filthy overalls had to be hand scrubbed and hand wrung before being hung out to dry, line after line. She worked obsessively, with frostbitten hands in Michigan winter's frigid blast, or garden wearied hands in summer's scorching heat and humidity.

Much less picturesque and attractive, on dark, drizzly, or sleet-driven Mondays, she would be forced to drape soggy underwear and wool socks over every door pull, chair and lamp-shade. Drying racks covered the floor registers. It was all part of the mom-job.

In her copy-cat-life, my mom could have sung the same refrain. She mirrored her mom's life in so many ways. *Add another log to the furnace!*

I remember it well, from a kid's naive vantage point, that is. How I wish, Grandma and Mom could have enjoyed a cheerful fireplace like mine.

My childish mind has no memory of Grandma (or Mom) ever complaining about the interminable workload of each and every day. Maybe Grandma's afternoon nap played a bigger role than we knew. Her bedroom door would close, and she would be gone to the world. When she returned, life for her and all of us was manageable once again.

It is a very good thing to turn back the pages of your life by taking time to browse through special moments and nearly forgotten events. Look deep into a photo for insight, or search out the meaning to a recurring memory that won't let go. Take time to write or journal your thoughts, and you will be blessed by the insight God gives.

Here's a writer's secret I am learning: The farther you open that squeaky door to your heart, the door you least want and may be fearful to open, the door with hinges squawking to be oiled or the lock refuses to hold, that is exactly the door that will lead you toward greater fulfillment. Let it swing wide open.

You will begin to understand more clearly, more honestly, who you are blessed to be in God's eyes and why He placed you where He did.

If you are not already grateful, ask for divine insight and perspective on the family and people who played a significant role in shaping you into the person you have become today. Learn, also, what is to be learned from all that is painful or tragic.

Forgive yourself and others who deserve, or don't deserve, to be forgiven. Forget the wrongs as you recall the depths of love and mercy God has shown to you. Then celebrate what is new today. Look closely. You will find God's Love is extravagant! It has no limits.

> *Reach out and experience the breadth! Test*
> *its length! Plumb the depths!*
> *Rise to the heights! Live full lives, full in the fullness of God!*
> —Ephesians 3:19 (MSG)

Something to Ponder

- Pull up some fond memories of a grandma, teacher, or special woman from your early years. What qualities stand out in her that resemble our Proverbs 31 woman?
- What special memories will you leave for your grandkids and/or family? How will others learn about your faith and your dreams for them?
- Use the gifts God has given you to share your love for others now. Be sure to leave a legacy of love for those around you.
- Read Ephesians 3:19 at the end of the essay. Have you been blessed to live in the fullness of God? Find ways to share those blessings in the Light of God's Word.

Time, Like an Ever Rolling Stream

The Lord will guide you always. He will
satisfy you in a sun-scorched land
and will strengthen your frame. You will
be like a well-watered garden,
Like a spring whose waters never fail.
—Isaiah 58:11

The world has impacted its message of obsolescence on our generation and, you might have noticed, even two rungs down the family tree where the grandchildren hang. We and they busily pursue the ghosts of illusion or delusion in what we wear and the latest tech toys we wished we owned or wish we knew how to use when we finally do own them.

Sadly, today's new model quickly becomes yesterday's vintage. There's no vision and no market for long-term maintenance. The next model or style is always so much improved and so appealing that it is humiliating to have anything but the latest. Time to get rid of the old relic.

A few months ago I met up with the biblical three score and ten villain of Psalm 90. A score, being twenty years, three score and ten is ... *voila!* I have arrived! Somewhere in time I never thought I'd be.

There must be something more I can do to avoid turning yet another leaf on a shrinking timeline! How did I get here? Did I think only I would live forever young, unaffected by the mortality rates of anyone I've ever known?

And why am I so apologetic? For breathing in precious air? Taking up limited space? Causing a negative effect on global warming?

Undoubtedly you have heard someone use the phrase, "Time like an ever rolling stream." It describes our inability to hold back the aging process in any lasting way. Penned by Isaac Watts, famous poet and hymnologist of the early 1700s, verse six of *O God, Our Help in Ages Past* is a melodic paraphrase of Psalm ninety that resonates through the centuries:

> *Time like an ever rolling stream bears all its sons away.*
> *They fly forgotten as a dream dies at the opening day ...*

Beautiful words, but the thought is stunning. It would be difficult to express the concept of constant change and aging with greater accuracy. Now that I am standing on this biblical precipice, however, *not* having this birthday seems far less appealing.

So with sudden insight, I choose to humbly (dare I admit, earnestly?) pray the time left is better than what verse ten of Psalm 90 proposes, that if we are strong we might see eighty but even then it's only trouble and sorrow.

(Must have been a bad day for the psalmist!)

So once again I have the incentive I need to head out to my walking trail. I'll try to beat the odds and cancel out a few bad carbs and sugars. When I return, I can assuage my conscience with a healthy snack. A bite-size dark chocolate sea salt caramel. Wonderful!

Now ready to move along, I pick up again in Psalm 90, to search for a better conclusion. Here it is in verse twelve:

Teach us to number our days so that we may gain a heart of wisdom.

Hmm! A heart of wisdom. That is exactly what I want!

Something to Ponder

- Name a few things you would like to see changed in the very needy world we live in.
- What keeps you and me from making the difference Christians are called to make in this hurting world?
- What thoughts come to mind as you think of your own life and how the years seem to gain momentum?
- God has given you goals and dreams to accomplish in your life time. Are you "on track"?

I Promise Myself

<><><><><><><><><><><><><><><><><><><><><><><><><><><><><><><><><>

From now on, there is reserved for me,
a Crown of Righteousness ...
Not only for me but for all who have longed for His appearing.
—2 Timothy 4:8 (NRSV)

When I turned sixty-five I decided to give myself a lasting gift, one that can grow and mature with time and never turn rusty or fall out of style or lose its value. It was a promise to be true to myself and to God who sustains me. Copy it for yourself if you agree.

I promise myself:

○ To be so strong that nothing can disturb my peace of mind.
○ To talk health, happiness, and joy to everyone I meet.
○ To treasure all my friends and family as special, loved, supported.
○ To choose to see only the sunny side.
○ To turn every negative into a positive.
○ To believe in myself and work to make my dreams come true.
○ To think and expect only the best.
○ To be as enthusiastic about another's success as my own.
○ To forget the mistakes of the past, mine and others.
○ To press on to my *high calling.*

- To greet each person I meet with a smile.
- To spend so much time on the improvement of myself ...
- That I have no time to be critical of others.
- To defeat worry, overcome anger, and live in peace.
- To stand strong and triumph over fear and evil.
- To live out the fruits of the Spirit— today.
- To step out for God boldly and audaciously!

Now I look back, after recently turning seventy-five. I had a few different goals then, but the core values remain. All of the promises I made to myself then are a part of me now, but I have not been conscientious enough about some of them.

How well or poorly I have kept these promises to myself is valuable insight into my spiritual well-being since each of them is reflected in my alignment with the One who walks with me, through every drudge day, every transition, and every celebratory day.

Something to Ponder

- How about taking time to make a list of "promises to myself." Feel free to copy anything that rings a mental bell for you.

CLEAN AND BEAUTIFUL ...
INSIDE AND OUT

There is not one blade of grass, there is no color in this world that is not intended to make us rejoice.
—John Calvin*

I remember thinking: if cleanliness is next to godliness, beautifying one's home, inside and out, must be a close runner-up. The creation story of Genesis 1 ends with, *God saw everything that He had made, and, Behold! It was very good*, or, in another version, *perfect*.

From our vantage point, God looked at all He had created, and *behold*! It was not only perfect, but it was incredibly beautiful. My reformed background reminds me that *our world belongs to God,* and we are its groundskeepers. Calvin took these words as a mandate for himself and us to maintain and create beauty in our homes and well beyond our doorsteps.

It is significant to note that Adam was given dominion over all creation before, not after, God breathed life into him (Gen. 1: 26). Care of the garden was pure joy until Adam and Eve fell to their own desires.

After that, they worked in the sweat of their brows to maintain what God gave them. They fought the weeds and bent their aching

---

* Quote taken from William J. Bouwsma, *John Calvin: A Sixteenth Century Portrait* (Oxford, Oxford University Press, 1988), 134–135.

backs to keep it in shape and to harvest a good crop so they could store their food to stay alive.

The garden of Eden was forever locked away from humanity and only a poignant memory remained. Our fallen parents lived with the sorrow of being disobedient and the knowledge that their actions brought sin and sadness into a perfect world only they had known and to the multiple generations that followed.

While I write this, a troubled teenager we know has just been in a terrible accident. Family and friends prayed often for him to turn his crazy, mixed-up life around. Now he awaits surgery and will be incapacitated for months.

Will he figure it all out and finally decide to make a permanent and positive difference in his life? His summer plans have been summarily changed, but God was gracious and spared his life.

We all have regrets. It's the story of our humanity. God often uses disobedience, misdirected anger, fears, and failures to draw us to Himself. We may look good on the outside, but sin metastasizes on the inside and will cause major damage if left unattended.

Only Jesus has the power to clean us up, inside and out, and head us in the right direction once again..

John Calvin concludes, "There is not one blade of grass; there is no color in this world that is not intended to make us rejoice."

Life will never be easy, but we have the power of the Spirit within to do great things and impressively more if only we ask.

> *For now you are light in the Lord. Live as children of Light,*
> *For the fruit of Light consists in all goodness,*
> *righteousness, and truth.*
> *Then, find out what pleases the Lord.*
> —Ephesians 5:8-9

Something to Ponder

- What's your reaction to these words: "Cleanliness is next to godliness. " Is your pointer finger on your outturned tongue, preparing to heave? Or, are you humming along with the message? "Yes, yes. I'm good with that*!" (Quote attributed to English preacher, John Wesley, in a sermon from 1778, titled On Dress.)*

- What is your reaction to the John Calvin quote at the top? Where is your spirit on this over-sized statement about God and all His creation.

- Are you questioning this guy's authority to make such an all pervasive statement about God or are you ready to jump right in and join Calvin in praise for the natural gifts and wonders, given to all, by the Creator Himself?

CLAY POTS AND BROKEN VESSELS

But, we have this treasure in earthen vessels,
so that the surpassing greatness of Power will be of God
and not from ourselves.
— 2 Corinthians 4:7

I'm reminded every day that we are merely earthen vessels. Our bodies break down with age, injury, or abuse. Our minds become foggy by reason of misuse, genetics, accidents, or stress. We make poor decisions that change the course of our own or someone else's life. *We're only human,* we say.

I was privileged to do a study of Gideon with Priscilla Shirer. An unknown in human history except for three chapters of Scripture, Gideon considered himself to be the weakest and least important of his family. This Biblical account is *all* about God's power perfected in Gideon's feebleness and the amazing things he was emboldened to do when he finally chose to obey.

Stop for a few minutes to read Gideon's true and amazing story in Judges 6–8.

Did you see the humor in God calling a doubter like Gideon *a man of valor?* Could you relate to Gideon's fearful request for proof that God was really God? And how crazy! That God chose only three hundred of thirty-two thousand willing soldiers to fight an army *as numerous as locusts* and with as many camels *as sand by the seashore.*

Think about the weapons God chose to put into the hands of this severely limited motley group of soldiers and their divinely commandeered commander. Trumpets and torches hidden in clay pots.

The story of Gideon is like reading a comedy. Laughable in so many ways. But God chose timorous Gideon to demonstrate His infinite power to His people and to the enemy. His tactics? Shattering noise and a rude surprise!

We are like those clay pots and broken vessels that God used to teach His people how to defeat their enemies and defend their faith. Our weaknesses become assets when he is invited to live His life thru us. His residency empowers us to do the impossible. Once He lights the fire in our hearts, we must keep it lit and stoked. The battle is won by following His instructions, no matter how outrageous.

It's uncanny what God can do with a willing soldier,
her broken vessel, and the blazing flame of His own fire.
—Priscilla Shirer, Gideon, 125

Something to Ponder

- After you read the story of Gideon's crazy adventure, what is your reaction?
- Do you happen, currently, to be on your own wild adventure, feared or excited? Try to put into words what your journey has meant to your life and/or others. (There's probably the good, the bad and the ugly, but find a way to focus only on the blessings you've found or been given, scattered along the way. Write them down for the rainy days ahead.
- Why must we be broken to be useful to God?

SHE SPEAKS WITH WISDOM

*So if you are serious about living this new
resurrection life with Christ, act like it.
Pursue the things over which Christ presides. Don't shuffle along,
eyes to the ground, absorbed with the things right in front of you.
Look up, and be alert to what is going on around Christ—that's
where the action is. See things from His perspective.*
—Colossians 3:2 (MSG)

The gurgling creek that runs beside her modest home brings fond memories of the love of her life gone on ahead. From her windows she watched her fisherman husband in his favorite spot and prayed blessings over him. This quintessential woman loved and always spoke highly of our fun-loving Uncle Ben. She is forever grateful for the sixty-five years they shared, but she lives for today, not in the past.

She has seen seventeen presidents come and go. Her face and her conversations are bright and filled with hope and good spirits. Her attitude toward life is positively positive. With memory sharp and intact, she remembers to inquire about concerns you shared the last time you visited.

I delight to hear her voice on the telephone. Her lilting *hell-ow-o!* pulses with her joyful attitude and the welcome conversation that is sure to follow. With God at the controls, she lives a truly blessed life and finds good in every single day the Lord allows her to stay with us.

This precious lady is known for her spritely ways and joy-filled thinking. At ninety-five she not only hears well, she listens well. Her eyesight is sufficient for reading her Bible and her favorite Christian literature. Her prayers follow a direct path to the throne of grace, but her personal requests are usually buried under a blanket of *thank You, Jesus!*

Gratitude pours from every pore, and she never hesitates to share that Jesus is her hope of eternity and that He is coming soon, at least for her!

Until recently, Aunt Ali enjoyed hosting her Bible study group in her home. She attributes her wealth of godly wisdom to living and staying close to the Lord. Her church family is nearly as precious as her own, and she continues to be a blessing as she soaks up the privilege of being able to attend services every week.

My aunt Ali offers profound but simple life lessons, sharing them freely. She knows many Scripture verses by heart and hums or sings the hymns and psalms of the past, staying focused in praise for her Maker.

As Christ followers we seek wisdom and aim to walk in its counsel. Aunt Ali was an important door to wisdom in my youth, and now I can enjoy seeing the abundant fruit of a life lived well.

She is the embodiment of the perpetually spring-time-fresh tree of Psalm 1:3, planted by the life-giving streams. She enjoys each day as one *whose leaf (or life) does not wither.* Her body may be failing her bit by bit, but her spirit has stayed fit and vigorous. As she prospers spiritually so have many others who have shared in the gifts of her legacy.

> *She is clothed with Strength and Dignity ... She*
> *speaks with Wisdom.*
> —Proverbs 31:25–26

Something to Ponder

- What do you admire most about my Aunt Ali?
- What are those gifts you'd really like to add to your life's story?
- Name some gifts you are currently pursuing in your own life?

LOVE THOSE IMPERFECTIONS!

I'm not saying that I have this all together, that I have it made. But I am well on my way, reaching out for Christ, who has so wondrously reached out to me.
—Philippians 3:12 (MSG)

Our preteens and teens are so deeply impacted by today's obsession with physical perfection and everything self-centered that the word *selfie* qualifies as just another cliché. Hair must be highlighted, colored, or textured and styled, nails professionally manicured and pedicured. Just like Mom's!

Tattoos are the envy and whine of twelve-year-olds. Face blemishes are reason to stay home to avoid ostracism, isolation, or total embarrassment. Bullying is at its worst. Suicide rates are increasing because, to a hurting child, suicide seems to be the easiest way to end the pain.

So how does one lost generation save the next as both appear ready to tumble over the cliff? Fixations on foibles or imperfections certainly restrict us all from any loftier thoughts than, *How do I look? How did I do?* Or, *What are my friends saying, (or thinking) about me?*

Young people are losing their moral compass to the insanity of *selfie-hood*. But, moms and dads are caught up in their own web of self-deception.

Women fight depression over normal baby weight gain and determine, at the cost of their overall health, to get back into skinny jeans and skimpy tees, to appear (yes, appear) fit and well-manicured.

Mandatory smart phone in hand, eyes and fingers flailing or mesmerized, dressed in up-to-the-minute work-out set and sexy sunglasses, they appear ready to face the day with confidence.

Is it surprising to see these moms push their young daughters to be all they dreamed for themselves, and her?

Sports and all types of fitness training are there for anyone with cash to spend. Kids, at a very young age, must be in all the right sports. Add to that, parents have to jockey their time to include the right fitness programs.

Family life revolves around endless practice schedules, games, and trying to feed with speed, often enroute. Sports and fitness take center stage and direct the weekly routines.

Sundays are punctuated with the same insanity, although now we try to add church attendance into the mix. Sometimes it works. Absorbing and assimilating the pastor's message or maintaining family devotions is near to impossible in this exhausting family lifestyle.

Togetherness? Eating McDonald's or subs and healthy snacks in the van, we are together. And on the road again.

Homeward bound, win or lose, we reinforce the coach's resounding critique, and then, the child's personal performance.

We determine to find time in an already shrunken schedule to make corrections *before* the next game. All this takes a giant's bite out of children's home life, play time, and subsequently, the family's well-being.

Dr. Oz, one of today's go-to gurus for health and beauty wisdom, urges women to accept themselves and allow themselves to be less perfect. Since Mom is usually the meal planner, carpool driver, and daily scheduler, it might be a good place to start, but there should be more.

Christians should have a radically different and much higher standard than any coach on the field. Fortunately, we also hold the key to unraveling what needs to be unraveled in our homes, and we have the compass for correcting course.

Nothing as important as this comes without cost. It takes a humbled spirit and a determination to intensify our personal relationship with God who alone can give us the future we envision for ourselves and for our children.

Beyond that, we might actually be the lifeline for a friend whose family is losing the same battle.

No matter how successful we are in making changes, know that God looks down with perfect love and affection on His most prized possessions. On us and our children, in all our perfect imperfections.

> *See what Love the Father has given us! We are called*
> *children of God; and that is who we are!*
> *Now all who have this hope in Him will want to purify*
> *themselves, just as He is Pure.*
> —1 John 3:1–3

Something to Ponder

- I made some bold statements you might like to react to. Are you offended? Aware and agree?
- What's most important as you think about building a great family heritage?
- Thankfully, God's standard of perfection is doable if we follow His lead and give Him our heart.

MOM AND THE PROVERBS 31 WOMAN

Charm is deceptive and beauty is fleeting;
but a woman who fears the Lord is to be praised.
Give her the honor she is due
and let her works bring her praise.
—Proverbs 31:31

My girls have many pleasant Grandma K stories, and I'm delighted for them. Our kids and grandkids sometimes share memories of the times she spent ironing at their own kitchen counters. It was her favorite way of helping her busy granddaughters with their little ones while giving herself a needed getaway from condo living. We all laugh together, remembering this one-of-a-kind lady.

When the sisters get together for lunch, we have another set of stories. Raised in the same household but with seventeen years between me, the oldest, and my baby sister, Deb, our stories have as many facets as the number sitting around the table.

Whether painful, amusing, or unearthed for the first time, each anecdote is valuable for understanding ourselves from another's perspective.

We always come away from our "counseling sessions" feeling grateful for the solid foundation of faith, hope, and God's love instilled in us by our parents.

We find so many reasons to celebrate one another, but we also appreciate what it took for Mom and Dad to raise a family of eight kids with the limited resources available to them. Dad and Mom loved each other, but life was pretty scratchy at times and not always kind.

Imagine: country girl with an abundance of responsibilities at home and eleven younger sibs in tow. She marries city boy, with one older, adoring sister and parents. He knows nothing at all about what it takes to feed, clothe, and educate a large brood. What would be the survival odds of that union? Particularly, as the numbers rise and the house and budget shrinks.

Fortunately for all of us, Dad was a fast learner. He morphed into a most diligent and faithful worker, and willingly handed over his entire paycheck to his penny-counting, country-gal wife.

God's grace made their life together possible, and their rewards came with knowing their children had followed in their footsteps with God at the center of their marriages and family lives.

In this tribute to Mom, I thought of the Proverbs 31 woman who is compared to a wife of noble character with value greater than rubies (vs. 10). We all want to be like that lady in Solomon's book of wise sayings. Yet, we are quite sure we fall short.

I remind myself of this virtuous lady and then decide to draw a few parallels between her and Mom. You may follow the episode in Proverbs 31:10–31.

- o **Her husband has full confidence in her, and he lacks nothing of value.** Dad pretty well trusted Mom to make the major (and minor) decisions for the family. He brought home the bacon. She fried it. He valued his wife and family above everything in life.
- o **She brings him good, not harm, all the days of her life.** Well, nobody is perfect here, but Mom was forever faithful to Dad and us.
- o **She selects wool and flax and works with eager hands.** It might have come from the thrift shop, but Mom only

purchased high-quality clothing, and when she sewed, it was done well.

- o **She burns the midnight oil** (paraphrased). Canning, sewing, mending, painting, wallpapering. Mom seemed to love the midnight hour. Did she realize like I do that her best productivity occurred when she worked with only God looking over her shoulder?

- o **She considers a field** (a farm, in her case) **and buys it, then plants and tends a vineyard** (or oversized garden) … and feeds the chickens, works an outside job, keeps a family of ten fed, healthy, and happy. Mission impossible for most of us!

- o All of, not part of, any extra income went toward Christian school tuition, but **Mom was willing to pay the price.** Anything it took to make sure her children grew up in God's vineyard.

- o **She works vigorously; her arms are strong for the task and she does not eat the bread of idleness.** Mom had two modes for living: work till you drop and sleep when you can't work anymore. The first won her best hours, hands down. No lingering over a morning cup of joe. *Loved it though!*

- o **She opens her hand to the poor and needy.** Always generous, a willing servant to the least. Her charities were her church, Christian school, Back to God Hour, and Bibles for Mexico.

- o **She is clothed in fine linen and purple.** Mom instinctively knew quality fabric and good style. She spent very little but dressed so well.

- o **Her husband is respected in the gates and he praises her.** Dad was loved by all, always proud of Mom, and not afraid to say so to anyone he met.

○ **She doesn't need to worry about the future.** Her treasures were heaven bound. She has received the fruits of her labor on the other side of tears.

○ **She speaks with wisdom and faithful instruction.** Her wisdom was practical and sensible and she counted on Christian teachers to fill in the gaps.

○ **Her children rise up and call her blessed.** It may have taken a while, but I can't imagine any of us doing better with what she was given.

Something to Ponder

- Recall a funny story or event, from the past. Talk about the bravery or courage of previous family members or friends.
- Next time you are together, make it fun and interesting for young and old to soak up the good Vibes and Vitamin C from telling stories till everyone is laughing or crying.
- Be sure, also, to tell good stories the young can pass along to their grand and great-grand kids.

FLOWERS FOR THE LADY

Flowers are a proud assertion that a ray of beauty out-
values all the utilities of the world.
—Ralph Waldo Emerson

In 1929, one hundred thousand tulip bulbs were sent from the Netherlands to be planted in celebration of Holland, Michigan's Dutch heritage.

Many early immigrants carried precious bulbs and seeds in their tightly packed trunks to ensure reminders of the homeland and to keep the promise of springtime alive in a new and foreign place. Soon, the merry month of May in Holland, Michigan, erupted with tulips and flowering plants all around town and a diversity of spring and summer flowers for cutting and display, like they were accustomed to in beautiful Holland, the Netherlands.

Flower gardens took center stage in most front yards, and carefully cultivated vegetable gardens were the pride and sustenance of many a family's food stock in preparation for hardy, cold Michigan winters.

Our Grandma Kraal loved her flower gardens dearly and was a proud owner of several awards given by the Holland Garden Club, where she enjoyed her role as one of the founders.

My mom's interest centered on vegetable gardening. With ten mouths to feed, there wasn't much time for flowers, but she loved them dearly.

Sister Judy surrounds herself with flowers at all times. In summer, most of them come from her own beautifully landscaped yard, and she holds many more awards than Grandma K ever dreamed.

All the Kraal girls love working with our hands in the soil, and our yards show that zest for living and love of ambience and beauty in and around our homes.

There is a viable dimension to the inquiry of why flowers speak to so many in so many languages. English critic, essayist, and reformer John Ruskin is quoted, saying, that *flowers seem intended for the solace of ordinary humanity.*

Floral displays, even before the bride enters, are usually the center of attention at weddings. At funerals, they are gentle reminders of the love and the life we shared and that this life is fragile and will someday fade as do the psalmist's flowers of the field (Ps. 103:15).

Almost any celebration has some sort of floral centerpiece. Flowers say, "Have a happy day!" Or "Have a happy _____!"

On occasion, we might hope to melt a cold heart with flowers that say, "I'm sorry, please forgive me." Flowers often convey what words cannot always do. In full bloom, flowers convey optimism and speak life.

Once again let me quote John Ruskin, that wise, old soul whose quotes live on for their foundational truths. He says in his treatise *Stones of Venice*, "The purist and most thoughtful minds are those which love color most." Can we invert that to mean that love of color, particularly in nature, can brighten and deepen our thought processes?

Holland Tulip Festival was firmly embedded in the fabric of my hometown in 1947 when city council decided to ramp it up for Holland's centennial celebration.

Mom, Dad, and I lived in Grandpa's "two-story" downtown when I celebrated my second birthday. I'm sure we were close to home when we watched the festivities.

As we continued to do, always around the time of my birthday on May 11, we attended the *Volks* or Peoples Street Scrubbing Parade on Wednesday, the *Kinder* or Children's Parade on Thursday, and wrapped it all up on Saturday with the *Musiek* or Parade of Bands.

A few years ago Holland celebrated an unofficial stemfest. If you know tulips, no explanation is needed. There had been bountiful tulips earlier. I remember hearing the DJs playing Peter, Paul, and Mary's "Where Have All the Flowers Gone?" I smiled a bit.

I remember another year that would have qualified as a budfest. *Que sera, sera!* Whatever will be will be!

Nelis Dutch Village, on the outskirts of town, invites thousands of visitors to step back in time to catch a glimpse of life in an 1800s replicated village in the Netherlands. Veldheer Tulip Gardens provides the greatest concentration of eye candy imaginable and, not to be forgotten, a trip to see the last windmill to leave the Netherlands in 1964 is the crème de la crème of Tulip Time: *De Zwaan* (The Swan) was reconstructed on Windmill Island and still turns rhythmically under billowy clouds of sapphire blue—at least in brochures and dreamers' dreams.

These festive celebrations continue to grow in size and duration, stronger and better each year, in weather that invites, delights, or sends townsmen and tourists into a tailspin.

Nearly a hundred years later, thousands of tourists still travel by plane, train, auto, or tour bus to revel in springtime's rare and sophisticated artistry of color explosion in my hometown. For several grandiose weeks in May, downtown Holland comes alive with music, dancing, tulip lanes extraordinaire, and the food of junkies.

Before the festivities end, the Veldheer and Nelis family and their staff reboot to welcome summertime crowds with all that is celebratory in Holland's present tense diverse neighborhoods. Their garden shops happily assist beginners and serious gardeners, all determined to revitalize their front and backyards with their favorite bulbs or seed packs.

A tweet from Jim Carrey, actor and comedian, shared a perspective that makes me look a little deeper into my own life when he says, "Flowers don't worry about how they're going to bloom. They just open up and turn toward the sun and that makes them beautiful."

Comparing myself to one of these created beauties, I find that it only takes a good watering of the Word, some dirty fingernails, and lots of Son-shine to go from dusty and dry to green and beautiful.

> *The wilderness and wasteland will be glad.*
> *The desert will rejoice and blossom.*
> *Like the crocus, it will blossom profusely and rejoice with*
> *shouts of singing.*
> —Isaiah 95:1–2.

Something to Ponder

- How do flowers speak to you in ways that other gifts can't? (Other than, allergies) ☺
- Flowers are often used for celebration and for remembrance of life and love, or heart-felt sympathy for loss. Celebrate life, past, present, and future.
- What is your favorite flower and why?

WOMEN'S WORK IS NEVER DONE!

*Let the beauty (favor) of the Lord be upon us
and establish the work of our hands.*
—Psalm 90:14

Grandma B's seven girls will clamor for acknowledgement when it comes to farm chores and heavy manual labor. What qualified as man's work was in no way limited to the males in the family and inescapable if you had hands and feet and muscle to lend during a busy planting season or harvest time.

We, girls, knew how to appreciate both sides of the workload! For some, the variety of farm-work and the fresh air of the barnyard was preferable to the mundane routine of housework.

Grandma would pull herself away from the big breakfast table by stacking plates and silverware. With a heavy sigh, she would quietly mumble, to no one in particular, "Well, on with the day. The pigs have left the trough!"

The correlation between smelly and filthy squealing pigs and my big, strong uncles didn't seem right at all to my three or four year old mind. True, they often smelled like barnyard, but they were not pigs, Grandma!

Another of Grandma's expressions, "a woman's work is never done," is actually a shortened version of the American Revolutionary idiom, "A man may work from sun to sun but a woman's work is never done."

I learned the truth of that colloquialism soon after I learned to walk and talk. Lessons in daily egg washing, hanging and folding clothes, washing and drying dishes, rolling oatmeal cookies, stirring cake batter, churning butter, or setting the table for up to fifteen. That, with no company present!

I remember it well, and yes, I love those memories. I actually learned to love women's work at this very young age. It represents most of my playtime memories, and I enjoy those same activities today. Well, let's forget about egg washing.

I don't remember a lot of conversation when I "worked with Grandma". It was probably her quiet example of conscientiousness that I admired and chose to emulate. As a young girl, the first time I heard the story of the Proverbs 31 woman, I immediately thought of Grandma B.

Who of us can know what it was like to be pregnant thirteen times and have to feed such a large and hungry family three times a day? Add to that morning and afternoon coffee time, which demanded some sort of baked goods. She had to be ready and waiting for the shuffle of boots and the scraping of chair legs. Five times a day!

Laundry for dirty farmhands never quit, and with only a worn handwringer washer and clothes lines for drying year round, one's imagination can hardly fill in the pieces of that living nightmare. Now think of vegetable gardening on a large scale and canning all you can possibly stash away for the dreary, long, and dreadfully cold Michigan winter. Truer words were never spoken: *A woman's work is never done.*

I never saw Grandma rush around crazy-like or scream uncontrollably as I would expect of myself or others of my generation in that never-ending routine. Somehow she trusted the Lord to fulfill her needs and those of her large brood, and He never let her down. No one ever left the table hungry, and the work somehow always got done, in God's time if not hers.

Something to Ponder

There were revolutionary (wishful) thinkers in Grandma B's family, but only on the women's side. None, on the men's side. Who had choices?

Several aunts definitely preferred the barn and the fields to the warmth of the woodstove and hot oven, the wringer washer with well-worn clothespins spread along clotheslines sagging under the weight of diapers, bib-overalls, sheets, blankets and towels, or those smelly, heavy duty socks! Those darned socks!

- Which would you have preferred 'waay back then' and why? Men's heavy duty farm-work or women's heavy-duty-never-finished-house-work?

REDEEMING THE PAST

And above all these, put on love, which binds
all things together in perfect harmony.
—Colossians 3:14

Life-changing events, sometimes outside our control, often create
the catalyst to encourage us to take one more giant leap of faith.

Going back to school late in life to become an elementary music
teacher, I had no idea of the long road ahead. Twelve incredibly
challenging years later I held a number of certificates and a BA,
survived four internships with teaching experiences from first to
twelfth grade in music, general education, and resource specialist,
K–12. I was fifty years old when I actually held in my hand a
Master of Arts in Learning Disabilities (M.Ed.)

Al chose that "yeah for us" moment to throw out another
challenge, "Let's go for a doctorate!" I had no trouble calling a
quick halt.

I wanted only to forget all that had transpired on the way
toward the accomplishment of a painfully protracted thesis. I
scarcely took time to open the black, hard cover with my name and
title in gold lettering when it finally arrived. Six full years earlier
I had birthed the resource program at CCHS for grades 9–12.

My plate was full, and my joy was based on my students'
success. *The Relationship Between the Academic and Social Domains
and Global Self-Worth,* by Anita Zuidema, M.ED sat forlorn on an

obscure shelf in my office, until this very day. I'll loan it to anyone brave enough to read the introduction.

As I started to write this essay, I reached for that thin but overweight tome. Supposedly, a copy is shelved in the stacks of my alma mater as well, but I'm doubtful the binding has ever been cracked, except maybe by another graduate student looking for relevant ideas finding only ancient stats. But today I shed happy tears as I rediscover something precious under the front cover of the book. I had all but forgotten for twenty years.

Just a simple congratulatory card, but the words touched my heart once again.

> *You should feel so proud. You set yourself a goal.*
> *You overcame all obstacles until it was achieved.*
> *Congratulations! Love, Dad*

Dad handed me this card when I graduated with a bachelor's degree in 1988. I think it was the first and only card I ever received from him, personally signed. Thank God I valued it enough to hold on to it. He was strong and healthy then.

Eight years later, in 1996, he had been gone more than a year when I regifted that message to myself by thoughtfully tucking it into this next milestone achievement.

Country singer George Strait has a marvelous song with poignant lines about a father's love being a "love without end." In the final lyrics he pictures coming into heaven feeling undeserving of God's love. Once again he is comforted with the thought that his heavenly Father's love for him is the best gift of all and stands tall as a true "love without end."

Something to Ponder

- When was the first or last time you took a giant leap of faith to leave the past behind?
- What happens once you make the decision to step boldly into an unknown future and move forward?
- Why was this new venture important to you? Were you assured of success from the start?
- How did this help or hurt you when the next leap of faith presented itself?

THE POWER OF LOVE

<><><><><><><><><><><><><><><><><><><><><><><><><><><><><><><><><><><><><><><><>

And above all these things, put on Love, which binds all things
together in perfect harmony.
—Col. 3:14

I have learned to summon whatever wisdom comes with increasing age to consciously live each and every day thankful that I live in this place with this good man. I only need to remind myself of the seasonal and daily weather changes that captivate my spirit and take my breath away to know how much I appreciate his forethought, his dream, to live on beautiful Green Lake.

What color shades of green will we see today? Are the waves gentle and soothing? Or are they dark and threatening? The changes from day to day and hour by hour never cease to allure the senses.

I'm opening my mail, sitting on my porch swing, watching a sailboat meander along the outer rim of the lake while a twosome of skiers challenges the wake behind an impressive looking MasterCraft, the one and only but unofficial ski boat of Green Lake.

On my lap is a special card that celebrates our forty-fifth wedding anniversary. In muted black and white, the front shows a backside view of a loving couple huddled together on a park bench overlooking a peaceful lake and a hazy skyline.

Are they young, middle age, or older than average? What are they contemplating? Growing children needing new shoes? Kids suddenly turned young adults, in pursuit of wrongful ... or lofty goals? A house finally sold? Retirement, and what could or does that look like, for us? Are they in a peaceful relationship or trying to pull it back together?

Are they quietly breathing in the beauty of a fading sunset? Does she appreciate the arm wrapped gently around her shoulders when chilly breezes stir or tightly when storms threaten on their life screen? Is he thankful for the mate God gave him to ford the journey ahead? Are they together now because they have learned from lessons in the past? Is there hope for the future and contentment in their togetherness?

These are the words as they appear on the front cover:
ends of the earth ...
> *out on a limb ...*
>> *over the moon ...*
>>> *places you'd never go*
>>>> *without Love to lead you there.*

The battles of human existence often wage war in ominous silence. Doubts and fears may crouch unseen and unheard in the cacophony of life while insidiously destroying from within.

At its fiercest, the battle erupts on the outside, noisy and strident. Then, another's hand and heart leads us back to safety and renewal. To have that *other* is a blessing the two of us have long enjoyed.

I'm thankful for all the places we've been together and the encounters I would have missed had he not pushed me out on a limb to experience the next crazy adventure. Love has led us to create something far better than either of us could have accomplished alone.

The inside of the card says:

Here's to the Joy of the Journey and to the Power of Love.
I whisper, "Amen" to that.

It is no surprise who chose this message for us. She has experienced the entire range of emotions possible on the spectrum wheel of life. Attesting to the highs and lows of marriage, brokenness, single parenting, children happy, and children sad. Together, she and the love of her life have overcome the incongruities and the beauty of a blended family.

She's gone the distance with cancer's deep wounds and scars. He lives with partial paralysis from a fall years earlier. They have lost much, they endure much, but the smile and the outlook on life is positively intact. Together, they have created an adventurous and openhanded lifestyle, a safe haven and a happy home for themselves and the family when they come to visit.

As soul mates, she and I have learned to savor the sweet scent of serenity. It's the joy of the journey and the power of love.

Something to Ponder

- Write about an instance where the strong arms of love held you tight during one of those storms?
- When there is no other person to hold on to in the midst of life's storms, The Savior Himself promises to be with us always and forever. Hebrews 13:5 says: *"Never will I leave you. Never will I forsake you."* If you need courage, love, rest, and peace, let these words echo in your heart.
- Then, you can add these words. *"I am His and He is Mine."* Take it and run with it!

FIELD OF FLOWERS

Where flowers bloom, so does Hope.
—Lady Bird Johnson

Grandpa B was gruff and farmer tough. He didn't play with us or hold us on his lap. I remember being completely amazed at a family photo of Grandpa and Grandma and the thirteen children. Pearl, the youngest, was actually sitting on his lap. Yeah for Pearl! Sometime later, she would become his valuable and loyal field hand, as "the boys" grew up and started their own farms.

Not a man of hugs and kisses, jokes or belly laughs. Smiles? Infrequent, as I recall. Was it the Dutch family tree he fell from? Hard to find more than a half smile in any of those rare photos. Or life, truth be told.

I still find it hard to believe he held such a fancy for flowers but he, good farmer that he was, was always on the hunt for opportunity, and he had waiting fields and farmhands to bring in the harvest. That's how Grandpa discovered gladiolas.

Beyond the normal livestock and cash crops of corn, wheat, oats, and hay, He expanded his knowledge on crossbreeding so he could more effectively market these beauties.

Soon a barren field in early spring turned into mesmerizing waves of brilliant colors in the heat of summer. The glads were a luxurious by-product of the far more valuable bulbs to be unearthed after cutting. Mail orders came from gardening companies across the country, a welcome income for Grandpa and Grandma's large family of fifteen.

Ahhhhhh! There's a real smile! It comes late in the evening, following a very long day. A broad grin overtakes him as he slowly elevates his tortured feet and yanks off his darned, forever darned, heavy socks.

I've often wondered why Grandpa B devoted his energy to gladiolus rather than tulips. It must have been a more sure investment at the time. Amsterdam probably held a tight rein on the market for tulips and a lot of other spring beauties with frequent flights scheduled to its offspring in Holland, Michigan.

Gladiolus were highly valued by Grandpa's ladies. Armloads of fragrant color brought new energy and sweetness to Grandma and Mom's living rooms. And what fun it was to sell these beauties on busy street corners to city ladies! Ladies! With money to spend! On pure frivolity! For us, empty buckets meant ice-cream cones for all. Yeah for frivolity!

I also recall a profusion of dinner-plate-size dahlias, a most addicting plant in the flower kingdom. I cannot be certain they were in Grandma's gardens, however. Maybe somewhere in the neighborhood or at the farmhouse we rented down the road.

When my sister Carrie married in mid-October, many years later, a local horticulturalist was ready to cut his field of dahlias. She had the wisdom to ask ahead, and we drove the morning of her wedding to gather a heaping carful of these dew-laden beauties.

Of the six sisters, no one had a more glamorous display of nature's color palette at their reception.

Then there were the majestic crimson, pink, and white crowned peonies, fertilized regularly with Grandpa's own organic cow manure in Grandma's side yard. Her giant, sweet-scented peonies, delightful dessert dish of the honeybee, nodded their frilly heads until they lost the energy to stand upright. Twine wrapped around the base of the burgeoning bush served to keep the majestic heads vertical. But nothing could match the joy of coming inside to see and smell the essence of these aromatic beauties.

One of the highlights of summer was gathering a bouquet of anything we could find that had bloomed. Wild, weed, or cultivated. The old house always took on a fresh look, and we savored the delicate perfumery.

I remember making dandelion tea with my aunts. "Dandey-lion tea", we called it. As I recall, only once. Lots of puckering, but no big smiles.

Kool-Aid. Now, that was a different story! How wide can you make a red Kool-Aid smile? Twenty-some years after it hit the market, that was our first choice on a hot summer day. More so, because it was so rarely served.

No sugar-free drinks then, but Kraal kids were used to Grandma K's heavily sugared tea, so no problem for us. Besides, none of us had an ounce of fat on our lanky bodies. The same was true for our Brink uncles and aunts. No need worry about a sugar high.

Most summer and fall Sunday afternoons were spent outdoors playing tag, softball, and croquet on the farm lawn. Big and little kids everywhere.

I always found myself more interested in the flower beds than in the games. Gentle breezes carried the scents of lilacs, wild roses, gladiolus, and peonies at different times of the summer. That might have been the reason we missed the overpowering smell of fresh spread manure or "garden honey."

On other occasions we would visit Grandma and Grandpa K in their small but beautifully landscaped city backyard. Flowers of every kind bloomed in well-designed beds bordering the entire yard for three precious seasons.

Most memorable was a giant blue mirrored glass ball perched at eye level on a cement stand and a bird feeder with actual birds flitting in and out and all around.

We would hold the little kids up to look into the ball to see a fattened-up version of ourselves. We would laugh and laugh some more. Soon it would be fancy cookies and tea time. Grandma always had windmill cookies and pastries from the bakery or *bakarei*. My favorites were the "deer leg" cookies and the "*krakelingen*", which we called "figure eights". How very special to kids who had little or no experience with anything not baked at home.

I received a birthday card from a farm lady friend today. I smiled and wondered who wrote this (at first glance) rough and unsophisticated poem. I'm ashamed to say, with all my years of schooling, I had no memory of the verse. See what you think!

> *When daisies pied and violets blue,*
> *And lady smocks all silver-white,*
> *And cuckoo buds of yellow hue ...*
> *Do paint the meadows with delight.*

My first thought? *Just shows that anyone can write poetry.* Wrong! Did you guess or did you know that William Shakespeare wrote this precious little gem? The verse comes from one of Shakespeare's earliest comedies titled *Love's Labour's Lost*. Google it and be delighted with Old World piety. Think Shakespeare's English garden.

Something to Ponder

- Am I too sentimental in this essay?
- What amazes you about each and every flower that grows?
- Who, but an infinite, beauty-loving God could have conceived of such an infinite array of designs, colors, and scents, bringing joy and beauty to the world He created?

MY SPACE

The lines have fallen for me in pleasant places;
Indeed I have a beautiful heritage.
—Psalm 16:6 (ESV)

When my mom died, about seven years ago, I chose to use my share of the inheritance money and celebrate her life by finishing off a well accoutered office just off the kitchen. Mom would have loved it! She did not like our balcony on that floor. "Too much wasted space," she said.

But Mom had never backed away from a paintbrush or wallpapering tools for a fresh, new look, so I know this tightly configured room would have met with her approval for practicality while satisfying her love of color and design.

Starting out as a home business office, it is now my favorite place for writing. It makes me happy knowing it was jointly designed and finished by my brother Cal and hubby Al. Cal's forte was building distinctive homes along the Lake Michigan shoreline, so I was pleased he agreed to work with us again on my little project.

The guys had worked together on several successful redo projects at our home on Blackhawk, so I was confident of good results. Both work intuitively and instinctively and respect each other's talents and ambitions. They are adept at envisioning the end results, excited by the steps to completion, and synchronize their efforts well.

Over the many evenings spent with us, Cal and I had a great time reminiscing and spending quality brother/sister time. Cal admitted mine was probably the most labor intense miniproject he had ever completed, but the results speak for themselves.

Al did all the painting, staining, and finishing of the maple shelving and trim and it is flawless. It was a great way to celebrate Mom and Dad's legacy, and we enjoyed the project and the time spent together.

From these windows I overlook tree-lined, scenic South Shore Drive. The three blue spruce that tower well above our thirty-foot roofline were set as small saplings soon after we moved to the cottage in 1990. Twenty-five years later, a variety of birds nestle into their piney branches, eye level to where I sit and muse.

Today, it is wooly white and stormy outside. The spruce are weighted down with more than a foot of snow, so Mr. Cardinal, fighting the junk birds in the feeder, is the only pop of color in view.

Whatever the season, I treasure my little retreat as the most precious space in my house, and when the time comes, I might just have to pack it up and take it with me.

Something to Ponder

- Where is your "my space?"
- Dream up a perfect plan for your own "dream space."

THE LAST LESSON OF CULTURE: SERENITY

For God did not give us a spirit of timidity or fear
But of Power and Love and Self-control.
—1 Timothy 1:7

It has taken too many years, but I have finally found the passageway to serenity of mind and spirit. Not a common word in today's relentless hustle and bustle, but deep inside every soul is a persistent desire and struggle to be at peace, to be calm and quiet in your inner person.

James Allen in his timeless book, *As A Man Thinketh*, gives this penetrating definition of serenity. I hold its message close to my heart.

Serenity is ...

> *That Exquisite Poise of Character ...*
> *The Last Lesson of Culture ...*
> *The Flowering of Life ...*
> *The Fruit of the Soul ...*
> *Precious as Wisdom ...*
> *More Precious than Gold, than the Finest Gold.*
> *Serenity Dwells in the Ocean of Truth ... Beneath the Waves ...*
> *Beyond the Tempests ... In the Eternal Calm.*

Did I actually say that I found the path to serenity? How is it, then, that I so often find myself lost in the thorn bushes, gathering scratches and bug bites, searching frantically for an illusionary wild rose of peace, convulsed in fear?

Did I stubbornly avoid or did I ignore the right path? Did I simply forget to follow the signposts? And what do I do now?

When I finally call a halt to my futile and frantic search mode and contemplate my actual circumstances, in the piercing light of God's Word and a heart-shaped prayer, then serenity comes and my heart swells with gratitude and renewed anticipation for whatever lies ahead. Its value has proven to be enduring for every set of circumstances and every season of life.

I am getting better at self-correcting my off course wanderings. In less time, thank goodness! The truth is serenity is never out of reach but a choice I must make each day. It is the choice to live by faith rather than fear.

Something to Ponder

- What are you drawn to from this essay?
- Meditate on these words, written by James Allen. What resonates with you?
- Did JA miss something? (Re-read 1 Timothy 1:7 top) If yes, what?

PREDATORS—NATURAL AND OTHERWISE

◇◇◇

The thief comes only to kill and destroy.
I came that they might have Abundant Life.
—John 10:10

One of my first assignments in a Create Memoir class was to write a short essay on my favorite place to spend time. From that diving board, I took a leap of faith and started remembering lessons learned in the place I had been two summers earlier.

It was past time to press back on all that was keeping me too busy to maintain my physical, emotional, and spiritual well-being. My self-defeating attitude was most likely the reason I felt zapped of clear thinking and joyful living.

I had ignored the signs of stress and lack of energy. I laid some of the blame on the shoulders of a hard-working husband who had no desire to retire and on circumstances outside my control. I was seriously lost and needed to find the way back to peace of mind and the healthy lifestyle I craved.

I began to consider my life as it was and what needed to change for me and in me. That difficult but healing summer opened the door into God's presence, where there is pure *joy ... with eternal pleasures at His right hand* (Ps. 16:11). It was God's hand that guided me, one step at a time, back to mental, physical, and spiritual health.

Many of us have spent time with the devotional *Jesus Calling*. A friend had given it to me earlier, not knowing to where I had fallen or did she? Sarah Young invites us to come into the presence of Jesus in every daily devotional. I started reading it that summer and have never taken the presence of Jesus for granted in my life again.

That summer, our trip to Ireland, was a perfect complement to the healing process that had begun in me. The pastoral scenes of rolling hills and kelly-green valleys that grace my screen saver today draw me back to an ancient land, a world away from where I hurry and scurry, learn and grow.

We drove miles and miles through shared pasture land with low-standing rock walls to delineate one farmer's sheep from another. Each farmer has his own unique branding iron to prove ownership.

But I wanted to ask, "What keeps the big, bad wolves from attacking? Shouldn't the walls be higher to keep out wild animals or other predators?" The bus driver, anticipating our unspoken questions, informed us that Ireland's sheep have almost no natural predators.

What would life be like without predators? Would we, could we be like those sheep grazing in a peaceful Irish green pasture with no concerns for our own well-being?

In our gardens, we have weeds and small or large animals that rob us of time, beauty, and homegrown veggies or precious plants. We are kept on the defense all summer. Farmers have to be on constant alert to protect their free-range cattle and fowl as well as their crops.

For those of us in city settings, consider having no moles in our manicured lawns, no weeds to pull, or crab grass thriving in dry seasons.

Technology's tools meant to assist and save time have become predators of the very things we value, our time and energy. In stealth mode, we are slowly pulled into the sticky web of technological wonders because we, much like our tweens and teens, simply must have the latest apps and bling, and we just have to keep up with the latest games, Facebook, Twitter account or blog.

At present, I am strongly being encouraged to blog with other writers to gain a wider audience. I understand the reasoning, but so far I have refused. I know how easily the hours mysteriously slip away, and I'm not convinced of the returns on my investment.

Several years earlier, I walked away from a career that required more dedication and time than I was willing to invest. Staying where I no longer belonged was painful, but I wanted to move forward, not just *on*. Caught in this conundrum, it was obvious that I needed to get real with myself.

Pastor Don recently spoke of *choosing to battle the temptations that lead to a divided heart*. What has more power to draw us away from our intended goals than our tech toys and apps? When given the choice of spending time in His Word or spending time with our brainteasers or mindless Facebooking with *friends*, who wins?

Predators must be recognized before they can be fought and neutralized or even destroyed.

Pastor Don used this verse:

> *Do not love the world or anything in it. If anyone loves the world, love for the Father is not in them. For everything in the world: the lust of the flesh (choosing the evils the world offers), the lust of the eyes (jealousy), or the pride of life (allowing ourselves to become the center of our own universe), comes not from the Father but from the world.*

—1 John 2:15–16 (ESV)

As I took steps to oust these robbers of my time and energy, I began to feel a new joy and passion for life, and that has helped me to focus on the freedom I now have to pursue new opportunities and ministries.

Today, particularly when I find myself wandering aimlessly, I picture myself as one of those contented sheep, grazing in a green pasture, peacefully serene, doing what I love and loving the life that has been returned, "in full measure, pressed down, shaken together, running over and poured into (my) lap."—Luke 6:38.

Something to Ponder

- What quiet, sinister, unsuspected, overpowering predators do we face on a daily basis?
- Name those predators in your home that you can't seem to oust.
- What will or what does it take to protect your family from these home-wreckers? (Re-read 1 John 2:15-16)
- Are you willing to go the distance?

What Goes Around Comes Around

<hr>

One generation will commend your works to another.
They tell of your mighty acts.
—Psalm 145:4

Our parents were eighth-grade graduates who worked manual labor all their lives, but Christian education was of primary importance, and they chose to pay the price with a lifetime of personal sacrifice.

With the hindsight of age and time, I am truly grateful, knowing Mom and Dad's sacrifice will make a difference for generations to come. They, and later we, relied on God's promise to His children when He said, "Love the Lord your God with all your heart and impress my Words on your children. Talk about them when you sit at home and when you walk along the way, when you lie down and when you get up" (Deut. 6: 6–7).

It was an every-day-morning-noon-and-night commitment. The reward is this: "In your seed all the nations of the earth will be blessed because you have obeyed my voice." (Gen. 22:18)

Today, our children have to find new ways to teach and train their children to be servants and ambassadors for Christ in a world spiraling down in moral decay. It may be that our grandkids will have peers who laugh in their faces and disparage their ideals, their moral convictions, and their choice of friendships and activities.

They will have to courageously stand apart in school, on the bus, in their neighborhoods, and on their sports teams.

It takes dedicated church leaders, parents and grandparents, friends and family, to pray daily for our children to be strong in the faith and willing to stand up or speak up when God impresses His Words on their hearts and minds.

Could I have imagined so long ago that being there for my kids when they came home from school and actively participating in school activities, endless fund-raising projects, bedtime stories and prayers would perpetuate in them the determination to do similar things for their kids? Probably not.

I thank God today for their diligence and persistence in paying it forward for the next generation. I pray their kids will want to do the same for my great-grandchildren, and theirs!

Something to Ponder

- Generally speaking, when do most people (you and me) appreciate our parents for what they sacrificed for us?
- Think quietly about what your parents contributed to your life when you were young. Be honest.
- How are you "paying it forward" for your own family?

Toward Endless Light

She unravels her life before His eyes, and then her own.
Retrieving, releasing simple and eloquent lore,
Buried deep in darkening tunnels of time.
She searches for threads that glitter and gleam
To tie up the prose of her life.

Bright threads to illumine the stonework
Of an invested, empowered existence.
Prized, rarer treasures blossom untamed
With pure and unabridged enchantment.
Still, she plumbs the depths of mystical shadows.

She probes the forgotten past with passion,
Conquering fear and lack of courage.
She awaits the promise of a loftier yield
And prays for eager souls to join the advance,
Toward hope and peace and restoring resolution.

Finally, she soars the heights of surrender
And journeys faithfully up the well-lit path,
With wings of prayer and grace.
Saints and sinners, as one, they converge
Together, walking on toward endless Light.
Anita Zuidema (01/01/17)

ABOUT THE AUTHOR

Anita Kraal-Zuidema was born and raised in Holland, Michigan, and earned her BA and MEd at Calvin College (now University). Anita is blessed to be married to Allan Zuidema, and they now live in Byron Center, Michigan, working to keep pace with grown and growing up grandchildren. This year we celebrate Carsten, our precious and first great-grandson. Together, we have hope for a bright future.

Anita writes to leave a legacy of words showing her love of family and friends and of God and His people. Her desire and prayer is that anyone who reads this book will say, "If she can do it, I can too!"

About the Book

She Walks in Beauty and Endless Light is a compilation of essays to celebrate the wise and virtuous woman of Proverbs 31, who has lived on through countless generations of grandmothers and mothers and is alive and well today! I am humbled to know many of these paragons of virtue. You will meet just a few in this small offering, but take heart—you will meet others in the next work already in progress.

There are numerous facets to this woman, but the golden strand that shimmers through the generations is virtue. The Proverbs 31 lady is a morally strong woman who radiates inner beauty, ambition, accomplishment, and godly wisdom. She has great value in her home, in the community, and everywhere she goes people are drawn to the light in her eyes and the wisdom she exudes. Her hands and feet are ready and eager to serve a needy world, and her heart is set toward the endless light of God's love.

If you enjoyed the book, tell others. You may contact the author through her website at anitazuidauthor.com.